HOW TO BAKE A
BUSINESS

HOW TO BAKE A
BUSINESS

*Recipes and advice to turn your
small enterprise into a big success*

JULIA BICKERSTAFF

ARENA
ALLEN&UNWIN

First published in 2009

Copyright © Julia Bickerstaff 2009

Arena Books, an imprint of
Allen & Unwin
83 Alexander Street
Crows Nest NSW 2065
Australia
Phone: (61 2) 8425 0100
Fax: (61 2) 9906 2218
Email: info@allenandunwin.com
Web: www.allenandunwin.com

National Library of Australia
Cataloguing-in-Publication entry:

Bickerstaff, Julia.

How to bake a business : recipes and advice to turn your small
enterprise into a big success / Julia Bickerstaff.

ISBN 978 1 74175 692 0 (pbk.)

New business enterprises--Management
Small business--Management.

658.11

Internal design by Seymour Designs
Set in 11/15 pt Fairfield Light by Bookhouse, Sydney
Printed in Australia by McPherson's Printing Group

10 9 8 7 6 5 4 3 2 1

For Mike, Henry, Edward and Charlie

CONTENTS

INTRODUCTION   viii

About me   x

If you can bake a cake, you can bake a business!   xii

How to use this book   xiv

Part I
THE BASIC BUSINESS RECIPE

1 Ingredients   6

2 Creating the picture   18

3 How-to-do-it steps   32

4 Equipment   41

5 Number of serves   47

6 The Basic Business Recipe summary   67

Part II
PROFIT: THE PROOF IS IN THE PUDDING

7 Pricing: the Steamed Syrup Sponge recipes   75

8 Volume: the Apple Crumble recipes   93

9 Costs: the Queen of Puddings recipes   106

$Part$ III

CASH: YOUR BREAD AND BUTTER

10 Cash cycle: the Basic White Bread recipes   **131**

11 Cash flow forecast: the Tea Bread recipes   **151**

$Part$ IV

TIME: HAVING YOUR CAKE AND EATING IT TOO

12 Free yourself up: the Chocolate Birthday Cake recipes   **169**

13 Free up your business: the Cupcake recipes   **187**

14 Buy help: the Christmas Cake recipes   **203**

$Part$ V

TIPPING THE SCALES IN YOUR FAVOUR

15 Getting results: the Weigh-Up recipes   **231**

LAST WORDS   **247**

THE PANTRY   **249**

ACKNOWLEDGMENTS   **255**

INTRODUCTION

When I first started working with 'kitchen table tycoons', Dr Tim Leunig of the London School of Economics was yet to come up with this delicious name for enterprising female entrepreneurs, and I was yet to become one.

I first started helping kitchen table tycoons by accident. Because I have a business background a friend asked me to give her a bit of help with her businesses. Until that time I had worked mainly with larger businesses—not *very* big ones but the sort that grow from $0 to $50 million quickly, raise equity, list on the stock exchange and employ lots of people.

I wasn't sure that I would actually be much help to my friend but I was happy to have a go—and between you and me, my 'nosey gene' wanted to see what she was actually up to!

I must have been of some use because she asked if I could help out one of *her* friends and, you know how it works, that turned into friends of friends. Now when I look back over the last five or six years I seem to have met hundreds—if not thousands—of women starting and running small businesses.

I have been enthralled with the type of businesses they are running: importing shoes, sourcing environmentally friendly gifts, producing organic shampoos, baking healthy biscuits, creating children's toys, making jewellery . . . the list could pretty much go on forever. And I was amazed at the number of these businesses beating big companies at their own game.

But for all the fun of having one's own business, kitchen table tycoons often tell me that the good stuff is tied up in a string of anxieties. And these seem to stem from either not having enough time to make the best of the business, or the business not making enough money to justify the time.

So I have been helping kitchen table tycoons change their businesses so that they can get more out for what they put in. And I have done this by taking some of the stuff that works well for big companies and stripping it down to something quite basic and workable for small businesses.

Recently, though, I was lamenting to a couple of kitchen table tycoons that I simply didn't have enough time to help all the women I would like to help. They suggested I write a book and so here it is—although as a side note I should add that writing a book isn't exactly a time-saving device!

So this book is for all women who want to follow their passion and nurture a business, who want to flex their creativity and create flexibility, who want to be mistress of their own time and their own success, and who want to build a business that suits their life and their aspirations.

This book is designed for women who haven't got time to wade through pages and pages of detailed advice, who know they need the nitty-gritty business stuff but would rather be out in the market winning customers, who need help to get the best out of their business rather than just information on how to structure it, and who know they don't need to know everything about business but do need to be on top of the essentials.

The aim of this book is to help you build your best business.

ABOUT ME

I grew up in England and took a degree in economics at the London School of Economics, London University. After graduating, I qualified as a chartered accountant with PriceWaterhouseCoopers, where I worked with many small and medium-sized businesses. It was a great time. I got to see inside all sorts of enterprises, including glamorous dress designers and modelling agencies, yummy chocolate manufacturers and cheese makers, TV companies and entertainers, and also the very-functional-but-not-quite-as-exciting manufacturing, property and import companies.

As everyone knows, London is full of Australians telling the English how marvellous Australia is, so in 1995 I thought I would see if this was true. I took a two-year sojourn to Sydney and forgot to go back.

My personal and professional lives started to mirror each other in 2000 when I became a partner at Deloitte (one of the world's largest accounting, consulting and advisory firms) and a partner to my husband. The years that have followed have continued in the same vein: my time is equally divided between helping small and medium-sized businesses grow, and helping small and medium-sized boys grow up.

Occasionally my family and professional lives have converged; my youngest son accompanied me to the filming of many episodes of *Kochie's Business Builders* (formerly *My Business Show*) and my older boys provided 'what-to-wear' advice when I co-hosted *Money Makers* on Sky Business Channel—Mum's dress sense, it seems, reflects on your street cred even when you are aged just five and six.

In 2007 I started my own business—The Business Bakery— so at last I can call myself a kitchen table tycoon too. I have learned a lot (which of course is a euphemism for saying that I have made plenty of mistakes) and my own experience is woven into the 'recipes' in this book.

My passion for helping kitchen table tycoons was accidental in conception and was nurtured in its embryonic form by friends who just kept on asking for help. But the energy to keep the passion alive has come from the contagious enthusiasm and infectious inspiration of every single kitchen table tycoon I have ever met.

IF YOU CAN BAKE A CAKE, YOU CAN BAKE A BUSINESS!

Incredible as it sounds, I am convinced that if you can bake a cake, you can bake a business. But why, then, do so many small businesses fail? Are they started by people who can't bake cakes?

Not exactly.

The way I see it is this. If you are going to bake a cake you need:

- ❖ to *want* to bake a cake—if you don't want to bake it, buy it
- ❖ ingredients—flour, eggs, butter, sugar
- ❖ heat—usually an oven!
- ❖ a recipe—something that shows you what to do
- ❖ equipment—simple stuff like a mixing bowl and wooden spoon.

And baking a business is really no different. You need:

- ❋ to passionately want to bake a business—if you don't want to build a business, go and get a job
- ❋ ingredients—all the stuff within you that's bursting to get out, like creativity, drive, commitment and desire
- ❋ heat—this comes from the enormous energy that you put into the process
- ❋ a recipe—something that shows you what to do
- ❋ equipment—just some basics like a telephone, computer and access to the internet.

You probably already have the passion and the ingredients to bake a business, and are prepared to apply the heat. But where do you find the recipe—the 'how-to-do-it' bit?

Most of us neither inherit the bake-a-business gene nor have the opportunity to learn it from our parents, and if that's the case then you need a recipe book. Here it is.

So, going back to my original question, do so many small businesses fail because they are started by people who can't bake cakes? Well maybe, but I think it's far more likely that they didn't have the passion, the right ingredients or sufficient energy.

Or a recipe book like this.

HOW TO USE THIS BOOK

Because this is a 'recipe' book, you don't need to read it from cover to cover, and you don't need to read it in order; you can just dip in and out of it as your mood—and your business—takes you.

This book is divided into several sections. Part I outlines the Basic Business Recipe. This is the one recipe that every kitchen table tycoon needs to be able to make. The idea here is to get to grips with the fundamentals to make churning out the fancier stuff so much easier. Think of it as learning to bake a simple sponge before turning your hand to a three-tier wedding cake.

Even if you have been baking for years, here's a little story with a big reason to read through the Basic Business Recipe section.

When I was a kid my mum made Summer Casserole every week and I loved it. Mum made it so often that she just did it off the top of her head.

I started to go off Summer Casserole though; after a while it just didn't taste so good. I eventually told Mum—not an easy conversation—but the upshot was that she partly agreed.

A few weeks later she made it again and I braced myself. But astonishingly it was back to brilliant. Bless her: she had dug out the original recipe and put back in all the special bits that time had left out. Thankfully, it would remain a regular feature on the dinner table.

Lots of people running businesses have Summer Casserole moments. The routine of the daily-do is so absorbing that it's easy to overlook the special bits that give the business its spark. So if you are already running a business I urge you to dip into the Basic Business Recipe section and remind yourself of the bits that make your business 'taste' so good!

Parts II, III and IV of this book are collections of recipes around a theme. Where a baking book might have sections on puddings, bread and cakes, this book has sections on profit, cash and time. If you are anxious about increasing your profit, for example, you can flick through Part II until you find a recipe that tickles your fancy.

Part V deals with weight management for your business and is all about results: there is nothing quite like seeing the fruits of your efforts to motivate you further!

And finally, The Pantry is a short glossary of useful bits and pieces.

THE
BASIC
BUSINESS
RECIPE

Here is the very first recipe to try when starting a business. It's a bit like practising biscuit making before going into mass production for the school fundraiser.

The Basic Business Recipe on the next page has the look and feel of a Victoria Sponge recipe. And because I am a great believer in feeding the stomach to feed the mind, I urge you to bake this simple cake and eat it while you read through all the chapters in Part I.

By the end of this section you will understand all the basics your business needs, and you should feel confident enough to experiment with the more elaborate recipes that follow in Parts II–V.

Here is our Basic Business Recipe.

	Business recipe	How to do it	Cake recipe
Name	Your business name		Victoria Sponge
Ingredients	Idea, purpose, passion	Chapter 1	225 g butter, 225 g sugar, 4 eggs, 1 tsp vanilla essence, 225 g self-raising flour
Picture	Vision	Chapter 2	Mouth-watering picture of a Victoria Sponge
How-to-do-it steps	Steps for how you are going to produce, distribute and market your product—and how long to do them for	Chapter 3	Preheat the oven to 180°C and line the base of an 18 cm cake tin with greaseproof paper. In a large bowl, cream the butter and sugar until pale, then gradually beat in the eggs and vanilla. Fold the flour into the mixture. Pour into the cake tin and bake for 25–30 minutes, or until springy.
Equipment	The stuff you need to support the making and selling part of the business	Chapter 4	Oven, mixing bowl, wooden spoon, scales, cake tin
Number of serves	How much money you are going to make/how you make money	Chapter 5	Makes 8–10 generous slices

As the chapters unfold in this section you will see that our Basic Business Recipe is simply an outline of how your business is going to work.

You might be thinking that it all looks very much like a business plan, but don't be put off. I too detest the whole let's-spend-a-year-writing-a-business-plan mentality. It's a complete waste of time—as are most 'how to write a business plan' courses. And please don't get me started on 'awards for the best business plan'. Two words on that one: don't enter.

So yes, it may look like a business plan, but this is the high-on-fun, low-on-formality version. And it's the one that works. Master it and you are well on the way to becoming a canny kitchen table tycoon.

quick bites

Do you just want to get stuck in? Can't wait to get started?

I'm certainly not advocating that you go overboard on the planning, as it is action that will get results. But a little bit of planning will help you prioritise, focus and potentially avoid a few disasters.

I wonder how many first-time cooks would forget to put on the oven before making a cake if it wasn't in the recipe? Covering the basics will help your business rise.

The *really* scrumptious Basic Business Recipe is:

- real—you actually intend to do it
- easy—the brilliance is in your *strategy*, not the written word
- costed—all the financial stuff adds up
- important—get the important stuff in first; the detail can fit around the edges
- possible—you believe you can actually do it
- exciting—if you don't get excited by it, no-one will!

quick bites

Perhaps you're thinking, 'What's the point in planning—something is bound to knock the plan off track.' Well yes, it is likely something will eventuate that you hadn't thought of or planned for.

But the real gold in doing a plan is the thought that goes into clarifying your intentions. Your detailed plan can be knocked about, but if your objectives are clear you will stay on course.

1

INGREDIENTS

A good business, like good food, starts with good ingredients, but what are they?

If you are baking a cake, four ingredients are absolutely essential: eggs, flour, butter and sugar. The other goodies (vanilla essence, cherries, icing . . .) are optional—nice to have, but not the end of the world if you don't.

The same goes for a business. Three ingredients are essential:

* a simple idea
* a purpose
* a passion.

The rest are just nice-to-haves.

You can manage business nice-to-haves in the same way that you manage them in cookery. If you are missing an ingredient you either do without it, or substitute something else in. Yes, the end result tastes a bit different, but it still tastes good—sometimes even better. A fruitcake without cherries is still a fruitcake, and banana bread made with plain flour and a spoonful of baking powder is exactly the same as one made with self-raising flour.

This chapter is about just the three *essential* ingredients because there is absolutely no need to get distracted by the nice-to-haves. It will help you check that you have got these essentials, and that they are in good shape. And *good* is all we are worried about here—not perfect. When you are baking a family cake you don't need the finest Italian flour—fresh in-the-pantry stuff is fine; you just need to check it for weevils.

Finally, like traditional baking—which simply doesn't work if you miss out the egg, butter, flour or sugar—you cannot bake a business unless you have all three of the essential ingredients. A brilliant idea without a passionate person to drive it will stay just that, an idea; and a passionate person with a less-than-brilliant idea will find themselves struggling with a fragile and unfulfilling business.

quick bites

You may be wondering why I haven't listed cash as one of the key ingredients. I do agree that *some* start-up money is important, but you simply have to manage with what you've got. If the recipe for your business calls for heaps of start-up funding and you don't have any, you need to change the recipe. This doesn't mean you can't start the business; it just means you can't start the business *in that way*.

The other ingredient kitchen table tycoons often worry about is business skill—or rather lack of it. Be assured that many great businesses have been started by people who don't have much in the way of business skills or experience. The best kitchen table tycoons recognise they are a bit short in that department, and one of the ways they manage this is to find well-equipped people to help them. More on that in chapter 14.

Essential ingredient #1: a simple idea

A simple idea is like an ice cube: very crisp, very clear and very cool.

What you need
❖ A simple explanation of your business idea.

What you do
Pour yourself a glass of iced water. While you sip it, write a one-liner that:
❖ crisply explains your business idea
❖ clearly explains who will buy your product
❖ coolly explains how you will make money from this business.

Now, because thoughts that sound perfect in your head tend to come out in a jumble when you actually speak or write them, don't just think about this, write it down.

Then talk about your idea to anyone who will listen. The more you talk about it, and the more you listen to what people say in response, the greater your idea will become. And if you are finding it difficult to explain your idea, it's probably because you haven't got it quite right yet. Keep working on it until you have a simple sentence—an answer to anyone who asks what you are up to. 'I'm starting a business that . . .'

And if, after all that talking, you don't think it's such a good idea anymore, bin it.

quick bites

Worried that one of your 'friends' might pinch your idea? Think about who you are confiding in. And remember what you learnt in high school: don't tell the skinny girl with big boobs and no morals about the hot guy you want to date.

quick bites

Sometimes you can be having a conversation with a friend about your idea and she just doesn't seem to get it. If that's the case, think about these points.

* It's easy to be negative, so make your friends work harder if they are pessimistic about your plans. Ask them to explain exactly what it is about your idea that troubles them. And get them to offer you some suggestions.
* Do they actually understand your idea? Maybe you haven't mastered explaining the concept yet.
* Do you agree with what they are saying? Maybe they know more about the industry than you do and they are trying to save you from disaster. Ask if they know any experts you could talk to.
* Maybe they are just not up to it. Sometimes the most amazing ideas are conceptually hard to grasp and you may just be way ahead of your friends (imagine iPod 10 years ago) . . .

quick bites

Not everyone is helpful. Here's a quick rundown of what friends say and what they mean:

'Really'—*'I'll believe it when I see it.'*

'It won't work'—*'No offence, but if it was going to work, wouldn't someone have done it already?'*

'That sounds really great, aren't you clever?'—*'Sounds dreadful but I love being your friend!'*

'How interesting'—*'Enough about you, let's talk about me.'*

Essential ingredient #2: a purpose

Sarah Tremellen started up Bravissimo because she was fed up with the awfulness of large bras. She decided that big-boobed women deserved something better than 'enormous matronly contraptions'.

This simple idea with a big purpose has seen her grow a mammoth, but elegant, business (see www.bravissimo.com).

What you need

❖ A purpose: a hole to fill and people who really want it filled by the stuff you are going to sell.

What you do

I like to think of purpose as the answer to the question, 'Who are you helping and how?' Completing the following statements should help you work this out.

1. 'MY CUSTOMERS ARE . . .'

Who needs or wants what you are selling? You might be tempted to answer this with 'everybody', but it's heaps more effective to find a nice bite-sized niche. After all, you are about to devote a large chunk of your life to understanding and looking after these people and we all have our limits. (More about this in 'Where are you going to play?' on page 22.)

2. 'MY CUSTOMERS ARE HUNGRY FOR ...'

What is it that your customers need *so* much that you have decided to leave your job/children/sanity to provide it for them? How are you going to increase the quality of your customers' lives?

3. 'AT THE MOMENT, MY CUSTOMERS ARE MAKING DO WITH ...'

If your customers are so hungry for what you are selling, what is keeping them from starvation right now? How are they possibly managing without you?

Put together an irresistible morsel about the need you are satisfying: 'My customers are big-boobed women, they are hungry for fabulous bras and at the moment they make do with tasteless over-shoulder-boulder-holders.'

Then taste-check your idea—ask a few potential customers what they think. Are they salivating or wrinkling up their noses?

Keep the answers to these statements light. This is just to see if your idea is good enough to take further. If it is, the next chapter—Creating the Picture—will help you fatten it up.

quick bites

We buy what we *want*, not what we need.

I am particularly proficient at this, having recently returned from a shopping trip with a new Karen Millen dress but no soy and linseed bread.

Apparently most of us have this syndrome. So for your business, think about turning the need for your stuff into a *want*. How? Talk about your stuff in such a compelling way that those who need it want it.

quick bites

The purpose of your business is not to make money.

Well, it is and it isn't. If you have a strong purpose and a well-run business then the money should follow.

But if money is your only purpose, you are set for disappointment.

Essential ingredient #3: a passion

Have you ever had an illicit affair? Been a modern-day Lady Chatterley?

I want you to think about an obsession that consumed you. An obsession that made you feel invincible. An obsession that drove you to do things you would never normally do. An obsession that divided you from your girlfriends, and was the sole reason for your existence.

Now you are getting close to the feeling that you need to energise your business. Passion.

What you need

✣ To feel obsessively passionate about your business idea.

What you do

Start by getting to know yourself. Ask yourself what:

✣ gets you really excited?

✣ are you dedicated to?

✣ are you obsessed about?

✣ do you love to do more than anything else?

✣ do you absolutely want to succeed at doing?

✣ drives you?

✣ do you want to change in the world?

✣ can you do to help people?

There is an important distinction between being personally passionate about something and having the passion to help someone else with it. I happen to think that many fitness trainers struggle with this. Many are only interested in their own bodies and are rarely that bothered about helping Mrs Tuckshop Arms tone up.

So look at your business idea. Does your business idea align with your passion? And does your passion align with your business idea?

If the answer to both questions is no, be kind to yourself. Think of a different idea. And use your passion as your inspiration.

quick bites

Love is blind. And as with a love affair, it is easy to get completely swept away by the passion you have for your business ... Don't let the passion for your idea stop you from hearing that your business is in fact a dud!

Precious Charms

Sometimes the best business ideas are those inspired by a lifestyle change.

Jaime Halward took maternity leave from her demanding corporate job to look after her new son. Having a bit of time up her sleeve, she also reignited a latent passion by taking jewellery-making courses. Returning to work part-time was an emotional period for her and gave Jaime the inspiration to craft a silver charm featuring her son's fingerprint so she could carry a precious memento of him with her.

Delighted with how the charm turned out she hung it on a necklace and wore it often. It became a great conversation starter; many people admired the charm, but few recognised it as a fingerprint. When Jaime told them the charm's secret they invariably asked her to make them one featuring their own child.

A business was born.

Jaime initially spent next to nothing on marketing but the business flourished. Customers fell in love with her jewellery and waxed lyrical about it to anyone who would listen. A successful business founded completely on word-of-mouth marketing has to be the ultimate proof of a good idea.

As Jaime says, 'To be able to leave the corporate world and set up on my own has been hard work, but so rewarding. It also means I can work flexible hours around my family, which is great. I love the fact that the emotional connection to your child's fingerprint charm makes it really personal and meaningful jewellery, and my business proves I'm not the only soppy parent around!'

And the business isn't just gold and silver charms for necklaces. Responding to customers' pleas for something for men (they are so hard to buy for!), Jaime has added a collection of cufflinks, and then for those for whom one of anything is never enough, there are key rings, chokers and bracelets.

Visit Precious Charms at www.preciouscharms.com.au.

2

CREATING THE PICTURE

The thing that spurs me into cooking is the picture of the finished product. Maybe it's my lack of imagination, but I do find it incredibly hard to drum up any sort of enthusiasm for a recipe if I don't know what it is going to look like when it is finished.

The photo in the cookbook may be the motivation to get you baking in the first place and the incentive to keep at it when the batter curdles, but how do you come up with a picture before you have actually baked anything?

You create a vision.

Now, vision is one of those business words that people get terribly hung up about. You needn't be one of them. It's just a mental image of what you want your business to be. It's that simple.

The way you create your vision is by taking your ingredients and beating them about a bit with some spirited questioning. This is fun and easy to do.

If you are thinking this sounds a bit on the fluffy side, it isn't. The best businesses have solid visions. And those that don't? Well, they sink in the middle.

VISION: THE PICTURE TECHNIQUE

To get your idea to rise into a business you need to fill it with vision. To stop it deflating you need to trap your vision and keep it locked inside.

You need the three ingredients from chapter 1:

❖ a simple idea
❖ a purpose
❖ a passion.

And five questions from this chapter:

❖ What do your customers look like?
❖ Where are you going to play?
❖ What does your business 'taste' like?
❖ What is your big business goal?
❖ What are your personal goals?

Then, write a short story about your business, its purpose and its goals. Don't worry about how you word it—just make it appealing and believable to *you*. And stick it on the inside of a cupboard door in your kitchen as an inspiring memory-jogger.

Try turning your story into a movie in your mind. If you want to get your jewellery sold in London's Harvey Nichols, imagine walking into the store and seeing it on display, or seeing pictures of 'It' girls wearing it in *Vogue*. And if you want to get your vision really locked in, grab some popcorn and watch the movie at least once a day.

Now I do appreciate this may sound a little crazy . . . but what can I say, it works!

Here's another thought. I have met many people who have started a business only to discover they didn't really want to run one after all. So take a look at the 'Personal goals' recipe on page 27, which will get you thinking about whether this might apply to you. Better to find out now than later.

quick bites

My friend Jo has a picture of a skinny bikini-clad blonde babe on her fridge. It's not a picture of Jo (you couldn't call her slim and she's very brunette) nor is it anyone that she knows. So why the picture?

Jo is trying to lose weight.

The blonde babe stuck on the fridge reminds Jo of her vision to lose 15 kg. A quick glance at the picture and she can block out the cries of 'eat me, eat me' emanating from her children's chocolate mousse.

Your vision will help you focus in the same way—but your husband might not be quite as thrilled with your picture as Jo's is with hers!

1. What do your customers look like?

The better you know your customers, the more likely you are to provide what they actually want.

If you were having people over for dinner I'm sure you'd go to the trouble of checking whether your guests are lactose, glucose or gluten intolerant, allergic to nuts, shellfish or eggs, or whether they are just having a vegan moment.

So, do you know how to cater for your customers?

What you need
- ❖ A few real customer-types that you can—metaphorically of course—undress and get to the bottom of.

What you do
Create a picture of your customer. Start by asking some questions. Here are a few suggestions; feel free to add your own.

- How old are they?
- Where do they live?
- Where do they work?
- How much do they earn?
- How do they spend their spare time?
- Do they have children?
- Do they drive?
- What do they read?
- Where can you find them?

Blend the answers together to produce a profile of your target customer.

Create or find a real picture of your target customer. Give her a name—mine is Amber—and stick the picture on your wall.

Whenever you are making a decision that will impact upon your customers, ask yourself: 'What will Amber think?'

2. Where are you going to play?

My children are young and consequently I spend far too much time in playgrounds. Fortunately we have plenty to choose from—unfortunately each member of the family has a different favourite.

You can't play everywhere at the same time—so where are you going to play, and why?

What you need
❖ A niche.

What you do
You are going to find a playground—a niche place to sell your stuff—and you want to:

❖ shape the playground by your rules
❖ pick somewhere where you can be number one or number two
❖ decide what your market share of that playground is going to be in three years.

You can make your playground whatever shape you want. And because you decide it, you define it. It doesn't have to fit into any traditional segments—and probably shouldn't. If you want to do 'mums of left-handed boys within a 5 km radius of my house', go right ahead.

The fabulous thing about picking your own playground is that it's like entering a competition and making up your own rules. If you can't win by the rules already in place, just start your own.

Picking a place where you can be number one or number two isn't about winning the 'my-toys-are-bigger-than-yours' competition. It's about upping your chances of success. If you pick a playground that is already crowded, the big girls and boys will be hogging all the good equipment and you will be killing time on the broken stuff.

It's hideously tempting to pick a massive playground. Blimey, why would you limit your business to one pokey little suburb when you could take over the world? There are lots of good reasons why world domination from a standing start is not the best option. Here are two of them. You would have to spend a colossal fortune on marketing to make even the tiniest impact. And one-size-fits-all stuff just doesn't.

3. What does your business 'taste' like?

Take a little 'bite' of your business. Chew it, bite it, roll it around your tongue, suck it and savour it. How does your business taste?

This is about the personality of your business and its essence, it is what makes doing business with you so delicious.

At birth your business inherited your personality, but if you need to you can change it!

And even if you don't want to tweak its personality, just think through the important bits of what your business stands for—then you can emphasise it, gloriously, to your employees and customers.

What you need

❖ A little note outlining the key flavours of your business's personality.

What you do

Ask yourself some questions about the business.

❖ What does it stand for?
❖ How do you want people to talk about it?
❖ How do you want people to experience it ('all the people are so nice to talk to', 'I feel cared for')?
❖ What are its really important characteristics (the things for which you would sack an employee whose behaviour didn't articulate them)?
❖ What is its philosophy?

Turn this into a few lines and write it down. It doesn't matter what words you use, as long as it comes from the soul of your business. Stick it up on the wall somewhere and, every so often, read it. Especially if you are feeling a bit cranky—I use it as a reminder when I'm feeling a bit 'less than'.

Feed and nurture your business's personality—your business can't be the best at absolutely everything, but it can be the best at who it is.

4. What is your big business goal?

This recipe is about giving you something to aim for, focus on and be inspired by. And, in case you need it, to give you a hearty kick up the bum!

What you need

❖ One big, measurable and almost—but not quite—impossible-to-reach goal.

What you do

Daydream a bit. Ignore all the practical stuff like not knowing how to grow a big business—just close your eyes and dream wildly. Feel the tingle of excitement as you imagine what your business could become.

Because daydreams suffer from the same affliction as night dreams—they evaporate as soon as you start to verbalise them—you need to write your daydream down. This simple act of writing will inject substance into your nebulous thoughts.

Colour your dream in. How many stores will you have? What will your revenue be? How many countries will you be in? How many people will you employ? When will it look like this?

And now translate your dream into a goal that can be encapsulated in a short sentence: 'By 2018 I will have 10,000 customers across the US, UK and Australia.'

Honesty is important here. If you want a big business, say so—there aren't very many accidental big businesses.

BUT I DON'T WANT TO DO BIG . . .

A big goal needn't mean a big business. A big goal is simply whatever you would really like your business to be. If you want a small lifestyle business, then set that as your goal.

Maybe your big goal is to have your business generate you an income of $100,000 a year but take only 20 hours of your time a week. Or maybe your big goal is to have your business help 1000 under-privileged children.

There's nothing wrong with small: it's the new 'big'.

quick bites

Worried that people will think you've lost your marbles if you tell them about your enormous goals? It's true that the more you talk about your goals the more real they become and the greater chance you have of success.

But don't talk about it if it makes you feel uncomfortable—sometimes things are better left unsaid.

5. What are your personal goals?

There is absolutely no point in cooking something you don't want to eat. Why cook pistachio biscuits if you can't stand nuts?

If you're not excited about eating it you won't be passionate about baking it; if you're not passionate about baking it, it won't taste good; if it doesn't taste good, no-one will eat it. So what's the point in baking it?

The most important person in the business is you. Make sure your vision is what *you* want.

What you need
❖ A bit of peace and quiet.
❖ A personal dream.

What you do
Start by creating a personal dream. My favourite way of doing this is to write a letter from the future.

Pick a milestone birthday, say 10 years away. Now sit down and write yourself a letter from the you in 10 years' time to the you today. You need to really get into the zone for this so you definitely need a bit of peace, and quite a few slices of Victoria Sponge.

Let your imagination run riot.

Start by thinking about where you are sitting (a fab new house? A new country? In your office?), what you are wearing (work clothes? A bikini?), where you are going today (school run? Gym? Your burgeoning business empire?) and so on.

Write it all down like a real letter. You will be amazed. The words will just flow out of your pen and you are likely to surprise yourself with what you write.

When you've finished, think about the business you are starting. How does that fit into your personal dream?

RedBalloon Days

You only have to meet effervescent Naomi Simson once to feel the passion she has for her business, RedBalloon Days.

One of the things I love about Naomi is that she tells the story of RedBalloon Days' first sale with so much enthusiasm you would think it happened yesterday, not eight years ago. Proof, if you needed it, that this is a woman who has revelled in every moment of growing a business.

Naomi started the business because she wanted to create something, and when the idea of selling *experiences* floated past her she grabbed it and set about building what is now a phenomenally successful company.

In part that success came because Naomi has an enormously positive personality, but it's more than that. She is infectiously positive in her drive towards her vision and her goals. Ask Naomi what her vision for her business is and without catching a breath she will tell you that it is to change the nature of gifting in Australia and New Zealand forever. Ask her what her big goals are and she will have answered before you have got your final words out. And that is what separates Naomi from the also-rans: she knows exactly where she is headed.

Naomi says 'success really comes down to what you set out to do and how you play the game to achieve it'. If you don't know where you are headed, how will you know whether you have been a success? She goes on to say, about starting RedBalloon Days: 'If I knew then what I know now—would I have ever started? The highs and the lows, the drama and the fun . . . life is vivid and I would not have had it any other way. To really appreciate the good times is to have experienced the tough times . . . adversity makes us stronger and more determined.'

You can't say it better than that.

Visit RedBalloon Days at www.redballoondays.com.au and Naomi Simson at www.naomisimson.com.

3

HOW-TO-DO-IT STEPS

*Y*ou've got the ingredients and you know what it's going to look like when it's done. But how do you actually do it?

From the blindingly obvious 'preheat the oven' to the ever-practical 'pour the mixture back into the rinsed-out saucepan', the best recipes are those that spell it out, step by step.

The how-to-do-it steps in this chapter are all about stuff—the stuff you sell. It doesn't matter whether you sell products, services or a combination of the two—it's all 'stuff'.

The actual how-to-do-it steps for your business are, of course, unique to you, and they are the magic that makes your business special. But there are three distinct types of how-to-do-it.

- How will you make it?
- How will you move it and store it?
- How will you serve it?

The purpose of this chapter is to help you think about all of them. If you only look at one or two you could end up with a rather lopsided business!

That said, depending on what you are selling, the 'how-to-make-it' could be particularly easy or really tricky. As I see it, if something is easy to make it is hard to sell and vice versa. So when you are putting together your how-to-do-it steps you will want to spend more time nutting through the hard bit rather than the tempting easy stuff.

My tip for creating your own how-to-do-it steps is quite simple: ask yourself lots of questions. It's often said of problems that we have the answers within us; we just don't always know the right questions to ask. I think this holds especially true for baking a business.

So, to start you off, over the next few pages I have included a collection of questions that I would like to ask you. This probably won't be enough, so you will need to think of your own questions too—ones that are special to your business. If you are finding this hard, ask your friends—in my experience they have a knack of coming up with the tough ones!

If you feel so inclined you may want to flick forward to chapter 10, which looks at the length of time your 'make-it, move-it, serve-it' takes, and why you want to keep it deliciously short and snappy.

1. **How will you make it?**

This is clearly the question that first springs to mind; whatever you are selling, you need a way of making it. It may be easy to make or hard to make, but the *need* to make it is always there.

An example of easy-to-make is bookkeeping. It's easy to learn how to do (if you have a talent for that sort of thing), but there are lots of bookkeepers so it's relatively hard to separate yourself from the pack and sell your services.

A haute couture Chanel dress is an example of hard-to-make: it takes countless hours to design, source materials, appliqué and sew. But the product is so exquisite, rare and beautifully branded that it is relatively easy to sell.

What you need
❖ A step-by-step plan for how you make your stuff.

What you do
Ask yourself these, and other, questions:
❖ What are you making?
❖ Do you have a formula you need to protect?
❖ Who is going to design it?
❖ Where are you going to get your raw materials?
❖ How are you going to make it?

- Will you make it yourself or outsource?
- Do you need to hire employees to help in manufacture?
- How much wastage will there be of raw materials?
- How much wastage of the finished stuff will there be?
- How many batches of stuff will you manufacture a year?
- What is the batch size?
- What new products do you need to design?
- Do you need to warranty your stuff?

It is, unfortunately, impossible to come up with a complete list of questions as businesses are all so different. This is where your nears and dears can be a great help; I am often amazed at the detailed and on-the-mark questions they ask. And I'm sure potential suppliers will swell your question bank too. Irrespective of who you are talking to, I think the most important thing is to keep your ears open for questions rather than just go looking for answers—or even worse, nods of agreement.

2. How will you move it and store it?

This is the how-to step that is most often overlooked. The whole bother of getting raw materials to the manufacturer, then getting stuff delivered and stored, is largely seen as an irritation or an irrelevance.

Which is a great shame, as this is where many businesses get themselves into a pickle. If it's not a garage bursting at the seams or a dearth of stock when the big order comes through, it's dollars sloshing around on thousands of transport invoices.

And it happens to businesses selling services as well. Think about the amount of time a bookkeeper wastes travelling between clients and how she handles having too much stock (her time) in October and not enough at year-end.

What you need
❖ A plan for how to move your stuff and store it.

What you do
Here are some more questions to answer:
❖ How will you get the raw materials to the manufacturer?
❖ What percentage of spoilage are you budgeting for?
❖ How do the goods get from the manufacturer to the warehouse?
❖ What are your insurance needs?
❖ What happens if stuff gets lost in transit?
❖ How's the stuff packaged?
❖ Do you need to customise your wrapping?
❖ Do you need a warehouse, or will the garage do?
❖ What security do you need over the garage/warehouse?
❖ How do you arrange the warehouse so you can find stuff when you need it and before it goes out of date/fashion?

- How do you get your stuff to the customer?
- What do you need to do to get good deals on delivery charges?

There really is quite an art to having all the right stuff in all the right places so that you can keep your customers happy without keeping you in hock.

Again, these are just a few ideas of questions; add your own flavours and toppings!

3. How will you serve it?

How do you dish up your stuff so that people will find it and consume it?

It's not enough to bake a great cake and expect the sweet smell of fresh baking to lure customers through the door. There are too many other people baking great cakes, and the fusion of smells has confused their noses.

So what are you going to do to find customers?

I honestly don't think it matters what you do to get customers as long as it works (turns into sales), is legal (jail is so not a good look) and you can afford it. And it's the last point that really throws a spanner in the works: sales and marketing can be deathly expensive.

So you need to be strategic, focused and plan your sales and marketing so that you get results without spending like crazy.

What you need

❧ A plan to get people to know about you and buy from you.

What you do

There are so many questions to ask here, but just to warm you up, here's a small selection (see also chapter 8, Volume).

❧ Who is your customer?

❧ Do you sell wholesale, retail or through an alliance?

❧ What does your customer look like?

❧ Where do your customers hang out?

❧ What are you selling?

❧ How do you sell? (Door knocking, website . . .)

❧ What does your packaging look like?

❧ Who will design it?

❧ How are you going to attract customers?

❧ How are you going to set your pricing?

❧ What sales incentives and promotions will you offer?

❧ What are your thoughts about advertising?

❧ What PR are you going to do?

❧ What sales people do you need?

I have been a complete philistine here and bundled sales and marketing together. If you want to be a bit more authentic, split this recipe up into: marketing (generating potential customers) and sales (converting them into actual customers).

Planet Cake

Paris Cutler's love of entertaining led her, somewhat quirkily, from the world of law to the land of *über* cake creation: Planet Cake.

This phenomenal business has not been without its 'how-to-do-it' tricky moments. First of all there was the 'how-to-make-it' challenge of turning seemingly impossible work-of-art cake creations into a business. Despite the fact that creativity and procedures make unlikely bedfellows, good processes turned out to be the answer.

You only need to look at the pictures on Planet Cake's website to see that the 'how-to-move-it' question must have been both tricky and expensive to solve. But solve it they did and now they send amazing birthday cakes all over the world—and they always arrive gloriously intact.

Their 'how-to-serve-it' piece has become multi-dimensional. Planet Cake is not just a cake creation place, it's an experience. An experience that cake-nuts who can't afford a 'couture cake' are just as keen to be part of as those who can. So Planet Cake runs cake-decorating workshops and an online shop and even has a 'cake fairy' who makes special visits to people going through a tough time.

With careful planning around the 'how-to-do-it' bits, Paris has turned a love of delightful novelty cakes into a truly scrumptious business.

Visit Planet Cake at www.planetcake.com.au.

4

EQUIPMENT

I once got halfway through a recipe and came to a grinding halt, stumped by an instruction to pour the mixture into mini-Bundt moulds. Mini-whats? Who said anything about needing one of these? I didn't have one and, judging by the way the little sponge things I was making turned out, the muffin trays weren't a good substitute.

This compact little chapter is simply about planning for the equipment that you need, rather than giving you a blanket prescription for it. It's like making a shopping list before you go to the supermarket so that you don't succumb to the dazzling array of unnecessary eats.

We're really not talking specialty tackle and tools here. We're talking more along the lines of general business paraphernalia. Stuff like websites, accounting systems and probably people— equipment that helps and supports you through the how-to-do-it steps of the previous chapter.

Importantly, you don't need a comprehensive set of chef tools in order to bake. In fact you can get away with next to nothing—having lots of equipment may make life easier, but is by no means essential. If you think about making a cake, you can do it using just a bowl, a wooden spoon and an oven. At least I think you can—I only ever use an electric mixer. I haven't got the stamina, patience and know-how to do it without the aid of technology.

And that's really the story with equipment for your business. If you can afford it, equipment is likely to speed things up (many hands make light work) and be more accurate (imagine keeping your accounting records by hand). Some of it, like an oven, is indispensable (a computer, phone).

You just need to choose whether you are going for the hand-held whisk or the electric version.

The key to equipment is to accumulate it according to what you actually *need*, rather than be swayed by what popular opinion says you can't live without. My favourite example here is a website. For lots of businesses a website is indeed essential, but many kitchen table tycoons have managed just fine with a simple blog until they need, or can afford to build, a proper site.

What equipment do you need?

While equipment can make life easier, when you're strapped for cash it can take on the mantle of extravagance.

But 'making do' is not always the answer—it takes too long, and your time is precious.

So there is a place somewhere in the middle for a small collection of well-chosen tools that, while not indispensable, certainly make your life easier.

What you need
* Support for you (both you the business, and you the person) over the next year so you can create and sell stuff.

What you do
Create a wish list of the equipment you would like in your business. Then prioritise these between the must-haves, nice-to-haves and sheer luxuries.

Don't consign something to the luxury bin just because it is terribly expensive; if it is imperative to your business, you may be better to have just that single piece of equipment than lots of cheap but dispensable tools in other areas.

Here are a few questions to help you think about equipment you might need:
* What premises do you need? (Home-based, or rental.)

- Do you need a website? (How will you develop it, who will host it?)
- Do you need help running the business? (See chapter 14.)
- What about accounting? (Who will do it, what package will they use?)
- What systems do you need? (See chapter 13.)
- What can you outsource? (See chapter 14.)
- What are your computer, telephone and internet needs?
- What do you need training in?
- Do you need to hire support people? (For example, an assistant.)
- What stationery do you need?

I like to grab a coffee and my imagination and think, if I had all the money I needed, what support I would like in my business. I find this little daydream cuts through the noise and pinpoints the equipment that will really make a difference.

Having the right equipment can be a real relief. It brings a sense of freedom. I love that things can be done quickly and properly—gloriously, with less effort from me!

Connect Marketing

Disenchanted with her corporate career, and facing a change in her personal circumstances, Carolyn Stafford decided to take the plunge and do something that she had planned for many years but somehow not quite found the right time to do: set up her own business. As she says, 'I wanted a lifestyle, I wanted flexibility to spend time with my young son, I wanted to be my own boss and, more than anything, I wanted to make a difference to people's lives.'

So Carolyn set up Connect Marketing to help small businesses be brilliant at marketing, and embarked on her personal vision of a life spent doing her three favourite things: speaking, writing and travelling.

Clearly the 'how-to-do-it' bit of Carolyn's business is the book she has written, the seminars and workshops she runs, the speaking gigs she takes on and the mentoring she provides. Intentionally, much of her work requires travel, so she needs the support of great equipment.

'When I was planning my business I looked at my vision and could see that there were two things I needed straightaway: a website and an assistant—a website to be my shopfront, and an assistant to look after the business during my trips away. In fact my assistant, Doris, has become more than that: she is my right-hand man; her support frees me up to do the work that I do best and she is totally indispensable. At first I wasn't keen on taking on an employee—I didn't want to manage people—but I'm lucky, I don't have to; Doris manages *me*.'

Carolyn lives by her mantra 'punch above your weight', and set up her business to enable her to do exactly that.

Visit Carolyn at www.connectmarketing.com.au.

5

NUMBER OF SERVES

I once made apple strudel for 48 people. By accident. I was thirteen at the time and saw nothing unusual in a recipe needing 36 apples, 3 kilos of sultanas and nearly 2 kilos of sugar.

We ate it for months and I have never eaten it since.

The magic of baking—turning ordinary ingredients (butter, eggs, sugar, flour) into extraordinary edibles—is all about chemistry. The best ingredients, the finest equipment and the cleverest how-to-do-it techniques amount to nothing if you stuff up the quantities. The 'Domestic Goddess', Nigella Lawson, said it herself: 'a cake demands mathematical respect'.

And baking a business demands mathematical respect too. Like it or not, a business is about numbers. It's about making sure that you get out more than you put in—in other words, it's about making a profit. And there is only one certainty. If you don't understand how your business is going to make money, it won't.

This chapter will help you work out how your business is going to be profitable, and because I absolutely appreciate that many kitchen table tycoons go cold at the mere mention of figures, it is designed for even the most hesitant number-cruncher.

quick bites

In the first year or so of a business it's quite common to find that you make a loss. This is understandable because you have to spend some money to get things going. But if you are going to invest a bit upfront, you want to feel fairly confident that the business will make a profit. And that is what this chapter is about: checking that, once the initial start-up phase is over, the business has a formula that's fruitful.

quick bites

Even if you are not in it for the money, you still need to make money. You might be running your business for altruistic reasons, but you won't be able to help many people if you spend more than you bring in. If you don't like the thought of a profit, just call it a surplus.

THE FINANCIAL FOOD PROCESSOR

What you really need is a food processor for numbers. Something you can chuck everything into, blend it all up and see what comes out.

The only slight spanner in the works is that you are going to have to make one of these wonderful little gadgets for yourself, and it's a collection of spreadsheets. But once you've made it, you can use it over and over again, so it's worth it. The marvellous thing is that if you don't like the taste of the mixture you've made, you can keep changing the quantities of the ingredients until you find a combination that works for you. Perfect.

So the financial food processor actually looks like a workbook of five interconnecting spreadsheets. If you have just turned a deathly shade of green at the thought of spreadsheets, please don't despair. They are just a tool. And I can assure you that you don't need to know any fancy techniques—just how to add up, multiply and link numbers between sheets.

The five spreadsheets are pages for five different types of data.

* Spreadsheet 1 is called 'Summary profit'. It shows the important stuff—how much you are going to sell and how much profit you are going to make.
* Spreadsheet 2 is called 'Revenue workings' and calculates how much revenue you will make.

* Spreadsheet 3 is called 'Cost workings' and calculates what your direct costs and overhead costs will be.
* Spreadsheet 4 is called 'Raw data' and contains all the 'real' numbers (for example, cost quotes).
* Spreadsheet 5 is called 'Assumptions' and is all the numbers you make up.

The following pages explain how you create each spreadsheet in the workbook. I tend to start with the summary profit spreadsheet so that I can get an idea of where I am heading, even though the numbers don't actually appear in this sheet until the very end. If you would rather start with the raw data and the assumptions then go right ahead. Do whatever feels right to you.

My advice is to just get stuck in and then it will make sense. Have a go at working through the spreadsheets. Do your calculations on the 'Revenue workings' and 'Cost workings', pulling all your info from the 'Raw data' and 'Assumptions' sheets, and link the answers through to your 'Summary profit sheet'. Look at the numbers flowing up to the summary profit sheet. How do they 'taste'?

To see how versatile your new financial food processor really is, take a look at the recipe on page 60, 'Feeling sensitive?' Finally, when you think you are done, take a look at the recipe 'How does it taste?' on page 62.

At first glance this financial food processor may seem like a lot of work. But it really is relatively painless—and anyway, a bit of effort now is more than worth it if it repays you with a business that has the right chemistry to be profitable. And tasty.

quick bites

Some stuff you need to know: profit is revenue less costs and is often called the bottom line because it's the bottom line on a profit-and-loss account (imaginative bunch, accountants).

Here are a few other basic terms:

- **Volume** is how much you are going to sell.
- **Price** is how much you are going to sell it for.
- **Direct cost** is how much it will cost to make your stuff.
- **Overhead** is how much it will cost to run the business.
- **Revenue** is your selling price multiplied by the number you sell.

USING SPREADSHEETS

These recipes are designed for very basic Excel skills. You can of course develop very complex business models with whiz-bang spreadsheet skills, but the more complexity you build into your model, the more room there is for mistakes.

Just do what suits you.

If you want some help with this, you can download a very simple model from www.thebusinessbakery.com.au.

If you are despairing about putting this model together because of all the spreadsheet stuff, get someone to help you. The spreadsheet is just a tool; the guts are in the content.

But please don't skip over this step as some business ideas just won't work out. So build a model to check yours out before diving straight in.

Spreadsheet 1: summary profit

This is it. The guts. The answer to how much profit you are going to make.

A little table that calculates a (hopefully) big number.

What you need

❖ A spreadsheet that summarises your predicted revenue, costs and profit.

What you do

You can breathe a sigh of relief, no numbers yet. Just an outline of what it's going to look like.

I have picked a fictional jam business to illustrate how the financial food processor fits together. This is not because I am an avid jam maker, but because jam making is a delightfully simple concept with just enough elements to give the example some life.

Set up your workbook to look something like the table shown here.

Strawberry jam: Profit for the year	$
Revenue	From 'Revenue workings' (spreadsheet 2)
Less direct costs	From 'Cost workings' (spreadsheet 3)
Gross profit	Formula (revenue less direct costs)
Less overheads	From 'Cost workings' (spreadsheet 3)
Profit	Formula (gross profit less overheads)

'From' just means that you pull the numbers from the 'Revenue' and 'Cost' spreadsheets; the only formulas are in the 'gross profit' and 'profit' lines.

As you haven't actually built the revenue and cost pages yet you will need to leave this recipe now and go and build those pages. Once you are done you can come back and complete this.

Spreadsheet 2: revenue workings

This little darling is the first of two spreadsheets that are simply about workings. This one is the workings for your revenue. It's a really simple, straightforward recipe, written for those of you who really cannot stomach numbers and calculations.

What you need

❖ You need to know that revenue is just the amount of stuff you are selling multiplied by the unit price.

❖ You need to work out how much of this wonderful revenue you are going to generate over the next year.

What you do

Set up a revenue template that looks something like this.

Strawberry jam: Revenue for the year	$
January	Formula (selling price of one jar of jam × January sales volume)
February (…etc.)	Formula (selling price of one jar of jam × February sales volume)
Total revenue for the year	Add the rows above

The formula simply takes the price of a jar of jam and multiplies it by the number of jars you expect to sell. The thing to remember here is that this page is just about inputting formulas. The formula pulls both the selling price and the sales volume from the final 'Assumptions' spreadsheet (that's where we will put all the numbers that we don't really know). So don't put any of your estimates in here—save them for the 'Assumptions' page.

If you want to build it up with more complexity (like different-sized jam jars selling for different prices), just add more rows until you have covered all your variables.

Just hang in there with me. It will soon make sense.

Spreadsheet 3: cost workings

Because data never comes in the way that you want it, this sassy little spreadsheet grooms the muddle from your 'Raw data' spreadsheet (#4) into elegance for your 'Summary profit' spreadsheet (#1).

What you need
❖ To work out how much your direct costs and overheads will be for the next year.

What you do
Set up a cost template that might very basically look something like the one on page 56.

In our jam-making example we want to calculate how much one jar of jam costs to make. The raw data will tell us the cost of 1 kg of sugar and 1 kg of fruit, but not the cost of the sugar and fruit per jar of jam. So we use this spreadsheet to calculate it.

Calculate the direct cost of one jar of jam		
Cost of sugar per kg of jam made	a	Formula (cost of sugar per kg × number of kg of sugar in 1 kg jam—these both come from your 'Assumptions' sheet)
Cost of fruit per kg of jam made	b	Formula (cost of fruit per kg × number of kg of fruit in 1 kg jam)
Total cost of each kg of jam made	c	Formula (total of the per kg costs above [a + b])
Number of kg of jam in each jar	d	Pull from 'Assumptions' (spreadsheet 5)
Total direct cost of jam per jar		Formula (kg cost of jam multiplied by the number of kg per jar [c × d])
Calculate yearly overheads		
Rent		Formula (12 × monthly cost from 'Raw data' spreadsheet)

If you want to build in more complexity—say, different-sized jam jars selling for different prices—just add more rows until you have covered all your variables.

With your overheads you want to come up with a formula for the yearly cost; this should be easy enough to work out.

Remember that this spreadsheet, like the previous 'Revenue workings' one, is only about formulas. Don't go putting any of your numbers in here. Save that for the 'Raw data' and 'Assumptions' pages.

quick bites

Direct costs are the costs that you only incur if you make a jar of jam—stuff that relates directly to the jam-making process or a straight-up-and-down delivery or selling cost.

Overheads are all the other costs that hang about, like rent, accounting fees, etc.

You can get yourself quite tangled up about whether something is a direct cost or an overhead. Don't bother. It just doesn't matter. If you think something is a direct cost, then treat it as one.

Spreadsheet 4: raw data

I'm a 'see-it, buy-it' girl, so window shopping usually vexes me. But this simple 'unshopping' expedition is actually quite fun—pretending to buy stuff we might need one day, just to find out how much it all costs.

What you need
- A shopping list of all the stuff your business will need.
- A smattering of chutzpah.

What you do
To make your shopping list, simply note down all the costs of your business under the two headings 'direct costs' and 'overheads',

then write down the names of people who sell this stuff (a couple of names for each).

Then call them up and get quotes. If the quotes vary drastically, get as much info as you can because you might want to explore, for instance, buying in bulk.

Remember you are window shopping, not buying. It's research, not retail.

On your spreadsheet, list all the costs and details so that it looks something like this:

Item	Cost	Unit
Sugar	$2	Per kilo
Strawberries	$4	Per kilo
Staff	$20	Per hour

Make it really simple so that you can just pull the numbers through to other spreadsheets. You need to be very disciplined here—numbers only, no workings.

quick bites

On your window-shopping excursion you will need to be thinking about size.

If you are a size 10 (i.e. you will need 10 employees to make your stuff), then you will need premises for a size 10, which will mean electricity for a size 10 . . . etc.

If, of course, you are a size 0 then a bijou home office should do just fine.

Spreadsheet 5: making it up—assumptions

You are simply not going to know the answers to some of your 'how much?' questions, so you are going to have to *make them up*. 'How much are you going to sell?' is the biggie but there will be other ones too.

The purpose of this spreadsheet is to keep a note of all the made-up things, or assumptions.

What you need
✥ To know what you don't know.

What you do
Set up a table in your spreadsheet and list all your assumptions. If you really were about to start a jam business there would be all sorts of quantities and sizes to make up such as the portion sizes and price, the number of batches to produce and the quantities in the recipe itself. So start a list of assumptions about quantities and sizes that looks something like this.

To make 10 kg of strawberry jam the recipe uses:	Quantity
Sugar	10 kg
Strawberries	20 kg
Time	5 hours
Size of jam jars	100 g per jar
Jam jars needed	1000
Jam jar selling price	$5

The truly wonderful thing about this table is that if you change your mind about an assumption (which you will—it's your prerogative), you can just change the numbers in this table and it will magically flow all the way through to your profit figure (well, it will if you have set up the formulas right).

Feeling sensitive?

After fossicking about for lots of raw data and imaginatively estimating how much of this stuff you are going to sell, you might be feeling a bit over this whole process. But now it's time to explore your stunningly versatile financial food processor and see how sensitive it is.

What you need

Play around with your assumptions to come up with three scenarios.

- The 'hope it happens' model.
- The 'far more likely' model.
- The 'it's a bloody disaster' model.

What you do

Basically you just add more or less of your ingredients, then taste the results.

Change your assumptions along the 'best case', 'most likely' and 'worst case' scenarios. See what happens to your profit and gulp.

Next have a look at where your break-even is. Break-even is where your revenue exactly covers your costs so you make a big fat zero. You don't make a profit but you also don't make a loss.

Take a look at how much stuff you need to sell to break even. Do you think you can do it?

SENSITIVITY AND VULNERABILITY

This sensitivity stuff is all about seeing how vulnerable your business is. Your business might be the sort where the bottom falls out of your profit if you just make a slight change to the amount you sell. That would make it very sensitive.

Conversely, your business may be a little insensitive (most likely if you have low overheads)—smaller sales may mean smaller profit, but not complete doom.

GOING ROUND IN CIRCLES

What happens if you do all the numbers and the financial food processor shows that you just aren't going to make any money?

You can do one of two things:

- Go back to the rest of your Basic Business Recipe and see what you can do differently.
- Give up.

And it does feel a bit like going round in circles—playing with the business plan, then the model, then the plan, then the model, then the plan . . .

How does it taste?

There is absolutely nothing wrong with a few surreptitious licks of the mixing bowl while no-one is looking—not doing so is a crime against the tastebuds!

But you do also need a proper taste test at the end. And by that I mean a nice relaxing sit-down with a plate of your (still warm) biscuits and a mug of steaming tea. *And* your financial food processor.

What you need

* To feel happy with the profit that you are predicting to make on spreadsheet 1 of your financial food processor.
* To understand what will happen to your profit if you change some of the assumptions (like you sell a lot less, or some of your costs are much higher).
* To be able to explain really simply how your business makes money.

What you do

Look at spreadsheet 1 of your financial food processor. What do you think of the profit? Does it seem worth the effort? Does it feel right? Do you feel (moderately) confident of achieving this? Do you feel excited?

Rustle up the 'Feeling sensitive?' recipe from page 60. What will happen to your business if your assumptions are a bit on the optimistic side? Will you be able to manage, or will it be blatantly untenable?

Explain very simply how you make money. Is it because you use locally sourced ingredients (pick your own strawberries) and cheap labour (uni students)? Or because you can command a fabulous selling price?

The ultimate taste test is the glow that comes from knowing *how* you make money, and knowing that you can, and *will*, make money. It's all about that beautiful big bottom . . . line.

Sheila Sunday

Doxia Dinoris didn't really intend to go into the biscuit business. It just happened that the biscuits she was selling at the markets, to raise some extra cash to put towards a holiday, were so divine that she was overwhelmed with demand. Fuelled by her success it seemed churlish not to turn this profitable little sideline into a business. So that is what she did. And, because the biscuits really were completely delicious, and probably as healthy and as tasty as a biscuit can be, she had lots of orders.

Before long Doxia was approached by a major distributor keen to sign her up for a big supply of biscuits. There was no way she could bake the number needed, so she would need to outsource to a manufacturer. This seemed like the answer to her prayers—the constant baking was wearing her down and now, with a big order on the table, she could get someone else to do the baking. So she ramped up her business, invested in packaging and the like, and then would you believe it, the distributor pulled out.

To recoup the costs of her investment Doxia needed to be selling big volumes, so returning to baking at home didn't feel like an option. But it proved hard to make money with the outsourcing model. As Doxia says: 'I did my business plan and my numbers on the basis that I was baking the biscuits myself and selling them at the markets; this way the numbers worked. But I should have redone the numbers when I started down the path of outsourcing production and selling wholesale. It was such a different model.'

Doxia was caught in a sort of no-man's land. 'I had a profitable business when it was small but I couldn't keep up with demand; then when I outsourced the manufacturing, the quantities I needed to produce to make it cost effective were just too big and I couldn't generate enough demand. There was simply no middle ground.'

Quite simply the numbers just wouldn't add up. So Doxia decided to close the business. Expecting her first child, and not feeling that excited about the business anymore, it seemed the right thing to do. But she says, 'I'm glad that I did it. I learned heaps and I don't rule out starting another business. But because the hardest thing in the early days of Sheila Sunday was having no-one around to talk to, next time I will talk to anyone and everyone in business that I can find.'

This story is the inspiration for the example in the pricing recipes in chapter 7. Oh, and the biscuits truly were scrumptious!

6

THE BASIC BUSINESS RECIPE SUMMARY

*S*o that's it—the five basic elements to help you build a recipe for your business and create a fabulous taste experience.

If you want to bring your business recipe together into some sort of document it's very straightforward. Just pull together a summary of your thoughts and workings from each chapter so that it looks something like the table on page 68.

This recipe is your plan for your business. It's possible that your accountant, or another busybody, might ask to see your business plan. Give them this. While your accountant might be expecting to see a more traditional format, the look of the plan is irrelevant. He or she will be *way* more impressed that you have a proper plan for the business—one which you are actually sticking to and which is getting results—than they would be with a 100-page 'how to build a business plan' creation that isn't what you are actually doing, or intend to do.

	Basic Business Recipe	Reference
Name	Your business name	
Ingredients	One line on your idea, and a paragraph on its purpose	Chapter 1
The picture	A short story about your business and its goals	Chapter 2
How-to-do-it steps	A summary of how you will do it	Chapter 3
Equipment	A summary of the equipment you need to run your business	Chapter 4
Number of serves	The summary profit spreadsheet (#1) from your financial food processor	Chapter 5

If your accountant (or anyone else for that matter) wants a business plan in a certain format ask them exactly how they want it. It won't take you long to turn your recipe into their structure because you already have all the info and have done all the hard work.

Don't waste time now though prettying up a plan. It doesn't matter what your plan actually looks like—nobody cares. It's all about action now.

RECIPE FOR THE YEAR AHEAD

It is also a really great idea to do a mini business recipe for the year ahead. This is a good technique for getting focused on what you want to achieve *this* year. And it will help you prioritise what is important because, despite wishing to the contrary, you simply can't do everything at once.

To prepare a mini business recipe you simply work through the headings of the Basic Business Recipe but with a view to what you want to accomplish this year, rather than in the wider future.

So, your ingredients don't change; your idea and purpose are the foundation of everything that you do. But you would change your vision—into a picture of what you would like your business to look like in twelve months' time.

The how-to-do-it steps will be how you make, move, store and sell the stuff this year. This could be a little different from the way that you envisage it in the Basic Business Recipe because in the first few years of your business you may be constrained—by cash or supplier credit—to make, for example, many small orders rather than a few big ones. Likewise, the equipment will be the equipment that you need for the coming year—and you are likely to find, when you run your financial food processor, that you will want to make do with as little as possible.

You will run your financial food processor using the guesses and assumptions you can make for this coming year. Irrespective of whether you do a mini business recipe, I have to urge you, as strongly as possible, to please run your financial food processor every year. It really can make the difference between running a healthy, profitable business and a basket case.

If you take a day out of your business once a year and think and plan for the year ahead, you will feel *so good* for it. What's more, your business will thank you for it—in profit.

$Part$ II

PROFIT: THE PROOF IS IN THE PUDDING

Often the anxiety about profit is not about how to make an enormous profit, but how to make a profit at all. Even those kitchen table tycoons who are making a small profit often lament that the money left over in the kitty is hardly worth the effort of running a business.

Irrespective of the overwhelming passion you have for your business and the undeniable need customers have for your stuff, you will only be able to continue running your business into the medium term if you are making a profit. To put it simply, the proof of your business is in the profit.

There are only two ways to improve your profit: increase your revenue, and decrease your costs. On the cost front, my guess is that you are probably being quite constrained around your spending as it is. So the emphasis here is on *managing* costs, not cutting them. Chapter 9 contains a selection of useful cost recipes.

The first thing the profit-hungry kitchen table tycoon usually thinks about is increasing revenue, and more specifically increasing the amount of stuff sold. Chapter 8 has a few back-to-basics recipes suggesting low-cost ways to increase the volume you sell. That chapter is deliberately skinny because, in my experience, most of you will want to devise your own special selling recipes—it's what you are interested in, and what you do well.

But there is another—often underplayed—way of increasing revenue, and that is through increasing your prices. I think, from my experience in the land of the kitchen table tycoon, that you are a very cautious bunch when it comes to how you price your stuff—and while that in itself is not a bad thing, you could be missing a trick or two. So with that in mind, the next chapter is devoted to making your business more voluptuous through attention to pricing.

Enjoy the collection of recipes that follows, but enjoy them more by indulging in the puddings described in each chapter as you go. So tickle your tastebuds while you add a bit of pudding to your business.

Steamed Syrup Sponge

Perfect for a cold day when you need a little extra comfort

WHAT YOU NEED

100 g butter

100 g sugar

2 eggs

175 g self-raising flour

2 tbsp milk

2 tbsp golden syrup

WHAT YOU DO

Grease a 750 ml pudding basin. In a large bowl, beat the butter and sugar together until fluffy. Beat in the eggs and gradually stir in the flour and milk. Spoon the golden syrup into the pudding basin and pour the sponge mixture on top. Cover the basin with greaseproof paper and steam in a saucepan of boiling water for 1½ hours.

Turn out onto a plate and give it an extra drizzle of golden syrup.

7

PRICING: THE STEAMED SYRUP SPONGE RECIPES

Syrup sponge is a combination that works perfectly. On their own the two bits of the pudding are a bit, how should I describe them, indigestible; the sponge is too plain and the syrup too sweet. But the amalgamation is absolutely wonderful.

There are also two discrete parts to pricing your product: the price that the market dictates (which I liken to the syrup), and the price that your costs demand (in my eyes, the sponge). And to be frank, neither bit is very satisfying without its counterpart.

Setting your price according to the market will guarantee a spike in sales—but not profit. If, as often seems the case, the price doesn't adequately cover your costs, you will come down to earth with a loss-making bump.

If, on the other hand, you set your price to cover your costs, then of course you should make a profit—but only if you actually make sales. And there's the rub. Laden down with costs, your stuff might simply demand a price that is too high for the market to bear.

So the recipes in this chapter are designed to help you balance the competing needs of the market and your costs. Go forth and be bold with your pricing, but remember that the Steamed Syrup Sponge is delicious because it is neither stodgy nor overly sweet. And if you happen to have forgotten how good this pudding tastes, make one, then savour it as you read.

PRICING, PLAIN AND SWEET

What you are really looking for is a comfortable nesting place for your price: somewhere in between the top price that the market will allow you to charge and the bottom price that your costs are demanding you charge.

But beware the pricing predicament: when your costs are telling you that you should be pricing above what the market will let you charge. Ouch. And it's more common than you would expect.

The recipes in this chapter are divided between those that look at the market's *sweet* view of your price:

❖ What is everyone else doing?

❖ What does your price say about you?

And those that look at your cost's *plain* view of your price:

- Direct cost per biscuit.
- Overhead cost per biscuit.

Plus a final one that melts the two views into one delicious dessert.

What is everyone else doing?

The good news is this stuff is fun, fun, fun to do. You just have to be a bit inquisitive. Or downright nosey.

What you need
- Heaped spoonfuls of delving.
- A dash of lateral thinking.

What you do
This is about finding out what the market is paying for stuff like yours. There's a veritable army of questions you can ask yourself, but here are a few goodies.

- Who is buying your stuff?
- What stuff can they buy instead of your stuff?
- Who is selling the competing stuff?
- How much are they selling it for?
- How easy is it to change between your stuff and their stuff?

❖ What is the difference between your stuff and the competing stuff?

If you devoured the recipes in Part I you will probably feel quite confident that you know what your customer looks like. But do you know how sensitive they are to price? Are they frugal or flippant?

And what stuff can they buy instead of your hot little number? This isn't necessarily a carbon copy of the stuff you are selling—it might just be an alternative. Tea and hot chocolate are alternatives to coffee, but they are each completely different.

So who else is selling? What sort of competitor are they? How big are they? Where do they sell? What is their cost structure? What will they do to prices if you put yours up or down? What do they know about you?

And how easy is it for a customer to change to your stuff from your competitor's stuff? Will you have to do something very special with your pricing to lure potential customers away from a tried-and-trusted friend or an arrangement they are locked into?

Then finally—what sets you apart from the competition? Is there something special about the experience that customers have when they buy from you? Do you have a special after-sales service, for instance? It all counts.

quick bites

It is easy to be a snoop because there is a mass of information out there if you just go and look. A good place to start is the internet.

You can also pay for specialist reports and for someone to do research especially for you. But I wouldn't bother.

If you want to do some special research, play dress-ups for a day and conduct your own. If you want to ask someone questions, go right ahead and do so. You will learn heaps more from having a conversation with a real potential customer than any report can tell you. And it will be way cheaper too.

What does your price say about you?

I am irrational. I recently stepped into a funny-looking boutique that I have steadfastly ignored for about three years. It's near the supermarket and looks like a junky sort of shop. Very not me. I don't know why I went in the other day but when I did I almost choked. The clothes turned out to be massively expensive and in that moment the boutique morphed into a *fabulous* shop. I bought three tops and joined their mailing list.

I do know I am nuts but, hey, so are your customers.

Price is how people determine the quality of your stuff. They can't tell whether it's good, but when they see the hefty price tag they assume it must be.

What you need

Answers to two really major questions.

- How 'elastic' is your stuff?
- How do you want your stuff to be positioned?

What you do

Whenever I think of 'elastic' I inexplicably think of knickers. But no knickers here, just a term to describe the impact that an increase in price has on the amount that you sell. If your stuff is very elastic, a small increase in price completely decimates your volume—and if that's the case, you will need to be devoutly careful with your price.

So you need to decide where you want your stuff to be positioned and then price it accordingly.

How do you want your stuff to be positioned? Manolo Blahnik heels aren't expensive because they cost such a lot to make (well, certainly not in materials—have you seen how thin the straps are?). No, they are expensive in order to keep the riff-raff out. If the hoi polloi are seen in them, bang goes their exclusivity.

At the opposite end are thongs. They are ridiculously cheap so that everyone can have *at least* one pair.

The fact that if you have a low price you are likely to sell more is not a startling revelation. But you have to sell *heaps* more if you have set a low sales price just to cover your costs. And managing enormous volumes is another story completely.

DON'T CHEAPEN YOURSELF

I am astonished at how much achingly gorgeous stuff is underpriced by kitchen table tycoons because they are not confident to whack on a decent price.

Fall in love with your stuff all over again. Write down all the reasons why your stuff is fabulous, stick it on the wall and remind yourself often. Don't cheapen yourself—you are way too good for that—and anyway, you don't win by being cheap.

ARE YOU TOO EXPENSIVE FOR THE MARKET?

Are you too expensive, or are you not giving enough value for the money? You may simply not be able to run your business if the selling price is much less . . . but you may be able to add *a lot more value* at not much more cost.

ARE YOU TOO EXPENSIVE FOR WHAT YOU ARE SELLING?

Charging a high price for complete and utter tat won't make you an instant millionaire. People will quickly realise that you sold them rubbish and they will kill your brand.

Price appropriately, not astronomically.

Direct cost per biscuit

There are some ludicrously good buys out there. They are not on the sale rack, they are not on eBay and they are not at garage sales. They masquerade as full-price must-haves, making them impossible to spot with the naked eye.

Sadly you will never know when you have bought one. Tragically, you may never know when you have sold one.

What am I talking about? I'm talking about people who sell their stuff for less than it costs them to make it.

What you need
❖ A good dollop of understanding how much your stuff is costing you to make and distribute.

What you do
Write down all the costs in your business that fall under the following headings: materials; manufacturing; packaging; and distribution and warehousing.

At the back of this book, in The Pantry, there is a basic explanation of what these cost headings mean—quite sufficient for this recipe. Oh, and ignore overheads for the time being.

Once you've got all your costs it's really just a matter of throwing them into the spreadsheet and seeing what comes out.

Set up a table that looks something like this (templates can be downloaded from www.thebusinessbakery.com.au).

Direct costs	Cost per biscuit
Materials (list them all)	10 cents
Manufacturing	100 cents
Packaging	5 cents
Distribution	1 cent
Warehouse	1 cent
Anything else we haven't thought of	
Total	117 cents

So in this example you would be nuts to price your biscuits at less than $1.17. Anything less and you are paying people to take your biscuits off your hands. Crackers.

Overhead cost per biscuit

We elegantly side-stepped the not inconsiderable matter of overheads in the previous recipe. Now we need to grasp them by the neck and deal with them.

What you need
- An estimate of your overhead costs for the coming year.
- An estimate of the amount of stuff you will sell over the next year.

What you do

Overheads are all the other costs of the business—the ones you have to incur whether you make a few biscuits or millions. They are costs like insurance, accounting, rent and marketing. The list can be enormous.

The broad idea is to work out an 'overhead cost per biscuit'. Think of it as sharing your overheads across all the biscuits you expect to make.

The *philosophy* is simple: if you estimate your overheads to be $100,000 and you expect to make 200,000 biscuits, then the 'overhead cost per biscuit' is 50 cents. It's the *estimating* bit that is hard.

On that note, your best bet is probably to flick back to the financial food processor in chapter 5, and then remember that a 'guesstimate' is better than nothing.

So how do overheads impact pricing? Well, if the overhead cost per biscuit is 50 cents then we need to add that to the biscuit cost in the previous recipe ($1.17), and we are now looking at a total cost per biscuit of $1.67.

If you knew that each biscuit cost you $1.67 you wouldn't sell it for less, would you? No. But if you didn't know the cost was that high, I wonder what you would sell it for.

If you have sampled these recipes and think your costs look way too high, take a peek at 'Costs' (chapter 9).

quick bites

I once worked as a Saturday girl in the chocolate department of a big department store. We weren't allowed to eat the chocolates, but damaged bits were fair game. A lot of chocolates got broken that year.

If broken bits are big in your business you might want to factor them into your costs.

quick bites

What if you're selling your services rather than a product? It works the same way, but you need to allocate yourself and your staff an hourly rate and then cost your services by multiplying the number of hours by your hourly rate.

I am quite wild about hourly rates, so there is much more on this subject in Part IV, Time.

Pricing—pulling it all together

This is a fabulously easy recipe to put together; it's just what you do with it after you have made it that's tricky.

What you need
❖ Heaped spoonfuls of the four earlier recipes in this chapter.

What you do

The biggie here is to look at the price the market says you can charge for your biscuit and compare it with the *cost* of your biscuit. Imagine the following scenarios.

YOU ARE AN EXOTIC BISCUIT AND CAN CHARGE $5 A POP

Looking good. With total costs of just $1.67 you are making a profit per biscuit of $3.33. Even better, because the profit is quite high compared to the costs you can be confident that even if your costings are a bit out it won't be the end of the world. Far from it. You have a nice bit of spare room tucked away there.

YOU ARE A CHEAP-AND-CHEERFUL BISCUIT AND CAN CHARGE $1 A POP

Oh dear. With direct costs of $1.17 you aren't even covering those. Stop right now before you do any more damage.

YOU ARE A MIDDLE-OF-THE-ROAD BISCUIT AND CAN CHARGE $1.80 A POP

Is this a good result? Unfortunately it's not as simple as that because of these two worries: the first is that your profit is quite small (13 cents), so if you have made any mistakes in your cost estimations then you could actually be facing the problems of the cheap-and-cheerful biscuit. This is even more of a nightmare because you probably won't even know whether your cost estimates are right until you get going.

Secondly, ask yourself: is it worth the bother? Take a look at the profit that you are going to make over a year and decide whether it's actually worth all that bloody effort. With the middle-of-the-road biscuit this is particularly important. Let's say you expect to sell 100,000 of them this year. That might seem like a great result, but when you consider that you would make a profit of just $13,000 (number of biscuits [100,000] × the profit [$0.13]) then you may well ask yourself whether it really is worth it.

COSTING IN SOME PROFIT

You might want to actually cost in some profit to help you work out an absolutely bottom price that you are prepared to accept for your biscuits.

Let's say your 'worth-the-bother' profit is $50,000. This is saying that you would be happy to slave over a hot stove and make 100,000 biscuits if you made $50,000 profit per year. You can cost this into your biscuits (at 50 cents a biscuit), which would mean your bottom line cost is now $2.17. You can then be pretty confident that, if you have done the numbers correctly and provided you sell enough biscuits, you will make enough money to compensate you for all that effort!

PRICING LOW FOR MARKETING REASONS

You may decide that you need to get lots of your biscuits into the marketplace and that to do so you have to lower your price for a short time. The new price will mean that you lose 10 cents per biscuit.

There is absolutely no problem with doing this as long as you understand how much it is costing you. If you know you will sell 1000 biscuits at this price then you know you will lose $100, and that $100 is a marketing cost.

It's only a no-no when you lower your prices in complete ignorance of the cost.

Sarah-Jane Shoes

In what sounds like the perfect job description, Paula Nemme flew from Australia to Italy for a four-week shoe-buying trip. The purchases were the initial stock for her online business, which sells fabulous ladies shoes for the larger foot.

One look at the initial price of Paula's shoes on her website though and you could have been forgiven for thinking they must have fallen off the back of a lorry. *Real* leather Italian shoes? It turns out they were the bargain of the century: the shoes were the real deal, but Paula had seriously underpriced them.

Says Paula, 'It was extremely difficult to establish a price model for our shoes because we were extremely naive. The light bulb didn't turn on until I started to look at shops which sold European-made shoes and realised that we were severely underpricing our product. Initially I found it emotionally hard to increase the prices, but as soon as we did it our sales volumes went up! It turns out that potential clients didn't believe we were really selling quality European shoes at those prices. Once we put the prices up there was a massive—and very positive—shift in their perception. After analysing the business model we also found out that we hadn't been factoring in a lot of hidden fixed costs, like storage and the really big one, my time spent working on the business—in effect I was being used as a free resource. I can still feel the anguish and trepidation of putting up our prices but it has been the best thing that we have done.'

Paula says she set up her business 'because I wanted women with big feet to be able to buy beautiful shoes'. And because Paula is now pricing her shoes properly, her business is flourishing and she can afford to continue to service this deserving market, for, as she puts it, 'beauty should come in all sizes'.

Visit Paula's website at www.sarahjaneshoes.com.au.

Apple Crumble

I can—and do!—eat this very often.

WHAT YOU NEED

CRUMBLE:
300 g plain flour
175 g brown sugar
200 g butter

FILLING:
450 g sliced apples
50 g brown sugar
1 tbsp plain flour
a pinch of cinnamon

WHAT YOU DO

Preheat the oven to 180°C. To make the crumble, mix the flour and sugar together in a big bowl and rub the butter into the mixture until it looks like breadcrumbs. Grease a 24 cm baking dish and spread the apples around the base. Sprinkle the sugar, flour and cinnamon over the top.

Top with crumble mixture and bake for 45 minutes. Serve hot with ice cream.

8

VOLUME: THE APPLE CRUMBLE RECIPES

*A*pple Crumble has to be one of my favourite puddings: easy to make, and terrifically delicious. Yet because it is such a basic comfort-food, it is often either completely overlooked or is meddled with to such an extent that you would need to be a culinary genius to recognise it as crumble at all.

I think we sometimes do the same thing to our selling and marketing.

Caught up in our quest to sell, sell, sell, we are often guilty of casting aside the basic comfort-food recipes in our desire to find a magic ingredient or technique that will propel us into volume heaven.

So, with the crumble recipes in this chapter I am urging you to go back to a few yummy basics which will comfortably fill up your business.

Basic is beautiful

When you are doing your marketing on a shoestring and are a sales force of one, you absolutely have to make the most of every customer you've got and every dollar that you spend. And that is the idea behind this crumble collection.

Here are four business recipes that really just serve as a reminder of how tasty the easy, everyday stuff can be, and how shameful it would be to discard them in the name of flirtation with more sophisticated—and expensive—methods.

- Sell new stuff to the customers you already have.
- Keep your customers coming back.
- Find new customers.
- Double dipping.

They require absolutely no expertise, they are completely uncomplicated—and, best of all, you can start making them right now.

Sell new stuff to the customers you already have

It's an exceedingly fine line. If you get it right it is very, very good, and if you don't it is unspeakably awful.

My hairdresser, George, does it almost imperceptibly by subtly wafting new hair-care products under my nose. Fast-food restaurants on the other hand do it brazenly: 'Would you like fries with that?'

It's called upselling.

What you need

❖ A generous understanding of your customer.

❖ Just a few *hand-picked* new products and services.

❖ Unbelievable care.

What you do

You simply sell new stuff to the customers that you already have, and you do it by thinking of what else they might like that you can sell to them.

Your customers are a captive audience; it is much easier and cheaper to sell more to an existing customer than it is to find a whole lot of new customers.

This is what hairdressers do all the time. They have the perfect opportunity to sell more to you. Not only are you sitting there for hours but they also have this perceived knowledge about your hair. So when they suggest that you buy some special (and ludicrously expensive) shampoo and conditioner that is *perfect* for your hair, you buy it. Hairdressers make a very good profit on the product they just sold to you; the whole upselling thing is an important part of their business model.

What can you do to sell more to your existing customers? Well, it depends on what they are buying from you. You may want to extend your own product range, or alternatively take a note out of the hairdresser's book and retail something that fits neatly with what your customers are already buying. You can be quite charming about the upsell. It's not simply about making them buy more—it's about offering them things that they really might *like*.

Keep your customers coming back

I am not really obsessed with hairdressers, in fact I studiously avoided them for many years after one too many awful experiences. But what I have learned is that while hairdressers may not always be great at haircuts, they are very good at selling.

What you need
⁂ To give your customer a reason to come back.

What you do
This is so simple it hurts: before your customer leaves you, rebook them for next time.

It may be a case of asking them when they would like to schedule their next delivery (because the delivery dates get very booked up . . .) or appointment (because everyone knows that streaks and colour are high maintenance and need topping up every six weeks), or simply just getting them back in the store (for 'special offer' week).

Rebooking is a service to your customer: it means that your stuff will just happen for them; they don't have to worry about remembering to book/order. And *you* get a customer that just keeps coming back.

Find new customers

The trick is not discovering yet more avenues to find new customers, rather it is about working out whether all that labour is actually worth the bother. Here is an unassuming little number to help you groom your efforts.

What you need
✢ To know what actions you are taking to win new customers.
✢ To know what revenues each of those actions generates.
✢ To work out how much each of those actions costs.

What you do

This is one of those recipes where it really is essential to check you have all the ingredients first. It is a recipe you will want to use over and over again, so it's worth getting the ingredients right.

If you simply haven't kept the right sort of information to date, never mind. Just start a little system for capturing this info from now on. Start asking your customers, 'How did you hear about us?' It's pretty inoffensive and it gets you the information you need for this recipe.

BASIC VERSION

- List the actions you are taking to win new customers.
- Alongside each action, note any external costs (e.g. advertising, marketing, consultant costs).
- Roughly work out how much 'you' time has been spent on each of these actions.
- Cost 'you' using your hourly rate (see chapter 12).
- If you have employees, cost their time too.
- Calculate the total cost of each action.
- List the revenues earned by each action.
- Calculate your return on investment (ROI). Return on investment is just revenue divided by the cost of generating it.

Transfer this information to a spreadsheet like the one following.

Action	External cost	'You' hours	'You' cost	Employee cost	Total cost	Revenue	ROI
Advertise in Yellow Pages							
Attend trade show							

If your ROI is less than 1 you are in a pickle. It cost you more to win the customer than they paid you in revenue.

If your ROI is 3, then you generated three times as much in revenue as it cost you to win the customers. And so on.

VARIATION

A more gutsy (but a bit more complicated) version is to replace 'revenue' with 'gross profit'. If you have calculated the gross profit on your product (your revenue less your direct costs) then you can use gross profit in the ROI calculation instead (gross profit ÷ cost of generating the income). This is so much better as the ROI then tells you how much *profit* you are generating for your efforts, rather than just how much revenue.

And as we know, the proof of the pudding is in the profit.

Double dipping

This little liberator is about doing things in such a way that you get more out for what you put in. How enchanting is that?

What you need
* Imagination.
* A little bit of courage.

What you do
Imagine that you are a fitness trainer and you make money by having one-on-one hourly sessions with your clients. There is clearly a ceiling on the number of clients you can work with in a week (168 if sleeping isn't your thing) and, of course, the money you can make.

If you want to grow your business and service more clients, consider the options below.

* You could train up a couple of people who can also work with your clients. In this model the client pays you and you pay your staff. Obviously you need to pay your staff less than the client pays you, otherwise there is not much point. And no, it's not daylight robbery—the profit you earn is compensation for finding the clients, training the staff and running the business.

* You could see more than one client at a time. This means that rather than train one-on-one, you train two people at the same

time. Even though you will probably need to reduce the rate your client pays per hour because they are now sharing you, as long as you don't simply halve the rate you will still make more money.

- A different variation on the theme is around how you 'sell'. Increase the amount of time you spend connecting with people who can refer you lots of clients (like the gym manager if you are a fitness trainer).

Pink Lily

Fed up with rummaging through her cupboards and being unable to find her shoes, or keep them dust-free and fresh, Sascha Griffin looked for and found the answer: stackable transparent shoe boxes. They were too good to keep to herself, so Sascha started selling them through her Pink Lily website.

The shoe boxes were an enormous success and Sascha quickly realised she had a dedicated following of women who were looking for stylish and practical products and who loved to shop.

So Sascha set about sourcing more products for her clients.

Fast-forward to today and Pink Lily is basically a glamorous mail-order business designed for the modern woman. The product range is diverse enough to extend to umbrellas, belt racks, perfume holders and cosmetic bags, and is growing all the time.

And while Pink Lily's customer list has also grown, the company's success started with Sascha's decision to source more fantastic products for her existing customers.

Visit Pink Lily at www.pinklily.com.au.

Queen of Puddings

This has been a family favourite forever—as kids, my sister and I would fight over the biggest bit. And I think, given half the chance, we still would. If you don't want to make the raspberry jam yourself, just buy it.

WHAT YOU NEED

RASPBERRY JAM:

500 g sugar
500 g raspberries

BASE:

275 ml milk
25 g butter
grated rind of ½ lemon
75 g breadcrumbs
2 egg yolks
50 g caster sugar

MERINGUE:

3 egg whites
1 tbsp caster sugar, plus extra for sprinkling

WHAT YOU DO

Preheat the oven to 180°C. To make the jam, spread the sugar on a tray and warm in the oven for 10 minutes. Heat the raspberries in a saucepan for a few minutes until the juices start to run free. Add the hot sugar and stir over a gentle heat until fully dissolved. Turn up the heat and boil steadily for about 5 minutes, stirring frequently.

Test for setting by putting a teaspoon of jam on a cold plate and leave to set for a few minutes in a cool place. The jam should wrinkle when pressed with a finger. Remove from the heat, skim off any scum and pour into sterilised jam jars. Seal immediately and store in a cool place.

To make the base, put the milk, butter and lemon rind in a saucepan and bring to the boil. Put the breadcrumbs in a bowl, pour the hot milk mixture over and allow to cool. Beat the egg yolks and sugar into the breadcrumb mixture. Pour into a greased 1.2 litre heatproof dish. Stand the dish in a roasting tin of hot water in the oven for 20 minutes. Remove dish from oven and spread masses of jam over the top.

To make the meringue, beat the egg whites until firm. Add the sugar and whip again. Pour the meringue over the jam; I like to peak it in the middle to resemble a mountain. Sprinkle with extra sugar and bake at 180°C for a further 10 minutes, or until the meringue is slightly browned.

9

Costs: the Queen of Puddings recipes

*C*osts are, quite simply, unpopular. There is a lot to be said for closing your eyes, clenching your fists and willing them away. But until that works we need a palatable alternative.

The problem at the heart of the cost conundrum is 'ignocence'—a blend of ignorance and innocence. Ignorance because you don't really know what is going on inside your business (usually because you aren't getting the information you need in a useful way), and innocence because you are a business virgin—you simply don't know what you don't know.

Now the discerning kitchen table tycoon knows that the way to boost her bottom line is through *managing* costs, not *cutting* them. And, despite what you may be thinking, managing costs doesn't have to involve a lot of effort. In fact, often the hardest part is simply psyching yourself up to do it.

My tip for getting in the mood is to start with a detour into the kitchen to bake a sweet and cheerily reassuring Queen of Puddings (recipe on page 104). For the uninitiated, this is culinary architecture: it's a base of sweet, sticky, spongy stuff, a layer of jam and a mountainous topping of meringue. It really is the *queen* of puddings.

Now you probably think I am as mad as a hatter. 'Bake a Queen of Puddings? Me?' Which is, of course, exactly the point: Queen of Puddings looks marvellously hard, but is actually very, very doable. You just need to take it one step at a time. Much the same can be said for managing costs. Looks impressively hard, but isn't—if you do it bit by bit.

The trick to managing costs is to get into bed with the enemy. Get to know your costs, appreciate their funny little ways, embrace them, and when you are really intimate with them, take a long hard look right into their eyes. If you don't like what you see, you are close enough to eliminate them. Painlessly.

The recipes for managing costs are a combination of the short, sharp and easy and some longer, fuller flavours. So take your pick and start where you feel comfortable. Oh, and the first four business recipes, when you put them together, culminate in a very useful sort of costs-out-of-control early-warning system. And the next four will help you save costs furtively but fruitfully.

COSTS—LOTS OF LOVELY LAYERS

There are three layers to the Queen of Puddings, and gloriously you don't have to get to grips with making all of them straightaway. If you just want to make one layer, you can—it will be eminently edible in its own right.

Same with your costs. The first layer, the eggy-bread base, is about understanding the types of costs you have and doing a budget. But if preparing the budget is standing between you and managing your costs, then skip over this and head straight for the meringue: know what you are actually spending.

And if the meringue is more than you can honestly cope with, just make the jam by taking a look at the 'saving by stealth' recipes.

Here's a breakdown of the recipes that will help you with each layer.

The eggy-bread base:

❖ Bundle costs together in groups.

❖ Budget your costs for the year ahead.

The meringue:

❖ Know what you are actually spending.

❖ Early pickle warning.

The jam:

- Saving by stealth—systems.
- Saving by stealth—bargains.
- Saving by stealth—do more of less.
- Forgettables.

While I readily appreciate that some of these recipes could hardly be described as effort-free, they are very satisfying. And anyway, do you want to beat your costs, or are you going to let them beat you?

Bundle costs together in groups

I do find that when costs are just lumped together into one great sticky mass it is really hard to work out what to do with them. And by that I mean I find it hard to work out which costs are too high and which are too low. (I know the idea that costs can be too low is a little startling, but it *is* possible to under-cater for things like insurance.)

So in my mind you can either squash all your costs into one massive plastic container, or you can divide them up into a few well-chosen, clearly labelled, neatly sized stackables. The latter, of course, are so much easier to find.

What you need

❖ An imaginary collection of containers in which to store and sort your costs.

What you do

Turn to The Pantry at the back of this book and flick down to the descriptions of costs. Think about the costs in your business and which container they would fit in. This isn't about blindly following an accountant's pro forma, it's about bundling costs together in a way that resonates with how you manage your business.

Don't worry if you haven't been looking at your costs in this way—it's never too late to start.

Budget your costs for the year ahead

A cost budget has got to be on your must-have list. It doesn't really take long to prepare and, once made, it's so versatile.

I do concede that the very thought of budgets can cause immense angst. But that's just because they have been demonised by accountants who expect budgets to be put together with an outrageous level of detail and accuracy.

Don't get bogged down by the nitty-gritty; think of it instead as an opportunity to play fortune teller and private investigator. It's only an estimate of what you think next year's costs will be.

What you need

⁂ An idea of what your sales volume will be for the year ahead.

⁂ Your budgeted costs for the year ahead.

⁂ A rough outline of which month those costs will fall in.

What you do

Quite simply, all you do is estimate the costs of your business for the year ahead.

To get in the mood, think about:

⁂ what your sales volume will be for next year, and what your business will need to look like to support that

⁂ capturing your costs in the categories outlined in the previous 'Bundle your costs' recipe

⁂ budgeting for the costs of your product along the lines of the 'Direct cost per biscuit' recipe in chapter 7

⁂ getting the information as accurate as possible without spending an inordinate amount of time on it

⁂ estimating in which particular month the expenses will fall.

The key to budgeting is 'just do it'. Spend a few hours on the phone getting quotes, review your expenses for last year, look at your financial model from chapter 5 and have a go. It won't be perfect but it will be boomingly better than nothing.

REMEMBER YOUR FINANCIAL FOOD PROCESSOR?

If you have worked up the financial food processor recipe in chapter 5 you will see that there are strong similarities between it and the budgeted costs. In fact, if you have recently done the business model, you should find the budget quite straightforward.

The financial food processor is a way of looking at your business to see if it can make money, whereas the budget is your prediction of costs (and revenue) for the year ahead. So the budget is more detailed and steeped in real-life expectations of the costs you will incur.

You can easily turn the financial food processor into this year's budget by setting volume as your target and costing it with estimates that are as accurate as possible.

Know what you are actually spending

I have been trying very, very hard to not notice how much money I fritter away each year on clothes. After all, if I am oblivious to the amount I am spending I can't torture myself about it, can I?

This is a terrible admission I know, but I can sort of justify it on the basis that I can't go too overboard on clothes shopping without my husband noticing—and let me tell you, that works as a very effective spending brake.

Funnily enough, though, I am exceptionally precise, bordering on downright tight, when it comes to spending money on my business. I absolutely know what I have spent and boy do I make sure I get my money's worth.

Being scrupulous is actually not so hard to do. You just need to know what you are spending in the first place, and that means keeping records.

What you need

- An accounting system.
- An accounting package.
- Useful coding.

There is an explanation of these delicacies in The Pantry.

What you do

Be diligent about keeping your accounting records up to date. If you have a nice little system for this then you will always know where you are up to with your costs (see chapter 13).

Be the boss. Don't let your accounting package get the better of you. You tell *it* what you want, not the other way round.

Code all your invoices really carefully. Getting your expenses under the right headings is the name of the game here, especially big things like direct costs and overheads. The more effort you put in, the easier it will be to interpret your figures and understand what is going on in your business.

quick bites

But what if you don't do your own accounts? Employing a bookkeeper is a brilliant move and one I completely recommend. However, bookkeepers can't second guess what you want, so you still need to tell them how to code the invoices so the reports give you the right info and you can manage your costs.

Early pickle warning

I have long been in awe of people who are good at budgeting their personal expenses. I was always a bit of a 'buy first, worry about it later' kind of girl and did pickle myself a bit in the process.

To pickle yourself in a one-pair-of-shoes-too-many way is fixable; to pickle your business is a different story altogether.

What you need

- ❖ Regular reports of your total costs to date.
- ❖ A budget for your total costs.

What you do

If all you do is a regular flick through your detailed cost reports then this is a step in the right direction.

But if you want a bit of an early pickle warning, try comparing your detailed cost reports to your budgeted costs.

- Every month, compare your budgeted costs with your actual costs.
- Investigate items where the difference between budgeted costs and actual costs is significant.
- Ask yourself whether you are spending too much or whether the budget is wrong.
- If you think the budget is wrong (it happens—it's only a budget), amend the budget and see what the impact will be on your bottom line.
- Think about what actions you can take right now to ease the pain of this increase in cost (for example, where you can make a compensating saving).
- If your costs are much lower than budget, check that you are picking up all your costs.
- If your sales are much lower than budget, think about what costs you can postpone until sales get better.
- If your sales are higher than budget, consider whether you should be increasing costs (such as taking on a new employee) to support those sales. What a startling thought!

Saving by stealth—systems

If you are being completely frugal with your business, as I imagine you are, simply whittling down your costs won't work.

So instead I am going to suggest another strategy: saving by stealth.

What you need
❖ Some good systems.

What you do
Imperceptibly, every day, profits ooze out of your business because of little mistakes and modest inefficiencies. But a few nice robust systems will slow down the profit trickle to a tiny drip.

Systems are just well-thought-out ways of doing things. If you have good systems, you won't have to keep reinventing the wheel and you also won't make as many mistakes.

You can have a system around everything that you do. It's nothing fancy—it's just the way that you operate.

A recipe for making a sponge cake is a system. Open any recipe book and there it is, a step-by-step guide to making a cake so that you don't have to work it out by trial and error.

You need to do the same thing for your business—lots of little recipes for how you go about, say, fulfilling orders, keeping your invoices and chasing your debtors.

It's a good idea to write down your processes. You don't have to do it in a particularly beautiful way, just in a way that makes sense to you.

I suggest you write down your systems and ask yourself:

- Why do I do that?
- Is there a better way?

And check out the recipes in chapter 13, which add a bit more flavour.

Saving by stealth—bargains

Until a recent—and very cathartic—clear-out, I could have taken you on a hilarious trip through my collection of unusual, unnecessary, unused and clearly unloved clothes. All bought for a non-bargain in the sales.

Whoever said 'a bargain is something you don't need at a price you can't resist' clearly had me in mind.

What you need
- To be wary of discounts.
- To embrace freebies.
- Swapsies.

What you do

Put your thinking cap on.

Obviously **discounts** are fabulous and should be taken advantage of, but only if they work for you. Volume discounts sound like a good deal until you realise how much you have to order—and pay for—to qualify for them; I know someone who got seduced into buying more than five years worth of packaging to get a good deal. She nearly lost the business trying to pay for it.

Everyone loves a **freebie**, so what can you get for free? Quite a lot actually. For starters, plenty of people will give you a bit of free advice if you just ask them. Most accountants, lawyers et cetera are happy to meet you for an hour or so before you formally sign up with them and that might be all the help that you need. You can also get all sorts of useful bits of information just by getting proposals from suppliers and talking to customers.

Promoting your business is something you can become very skilful at doing for free. Media articles, appearing on television shows and the like are all free and just take a bit of chutzpah. I have met great kitchen table tycoons who have had air time talking about their business on TV and radio, and if you ask them how they managed it they will tell you, 'I just asked'.

Swapsies: can you do a freebie swap with someone? The best kitchen table tycoons I know buddy up with their peers in different industries and help each other. Okay, you need to make sure it's worth your time because while you are helping your pal out you are not generating revenue for your business. But you get low-cost great advice and you will always get something you didn't bargain for—a bit of inspiration or a sassy little idea—thrown in too.

Saving by stealth—do more of less

My youngest son goes to daycare on the top level of a shopping centre, four very distracting floors up from the supermarket. The trip between the two means I have to walk past an enticing department store, a bookshop I adore and a treasure-trove of clothing emporiums.

Needless to say, I rarely make the trip from daycare to the supermarket without picking up a little something that I neither planned for nor needed.

And, albeit in a different way, it is surprisingly easy to pick up some quite unnecessary additions to your business too.

What you need
- Clear objectives.
- Some discipline.

What you do

I have absolutely no doubt that opportunities are tumbling through your door and of course you want to soak them all up. But it is hopelessly easy to find yourself frittering away your time and money on these enticing but ultimately unworthy distractions.

To keep yourself—and your spending—focused, do a little checklist so that you can evaluate each opportunity unemotionally.

Here are some questions you might want to think about:

- Will it help to achieve my short-term or long-term goals?
- Would I have searched this opportunity out?
- If I take this opportunity, what will I need to stop doing to make time or money for this?
- What will the financial outcome be, and how does this compare with the return I would get for using my time/money in a different way?

The key here is to stop spreading yourself too thin. Undoubtedly the more projects you take on, the less efficient you are likely to be. It's so much better to do one thing properly—so go on, invest in the biggest bang for your buck!

Forgettables

It's not just wishful thinking—some costs are actually very forgettable.

These are the costs no-one sends you an invoice for and no-one chases payment of, so you never record them in your accounting system.

Sounds perfect—a whole lot of work for nothing.

Except it's not really for nothing, because the person who doesn't send in an invoice is your most expensive employee. *You*. And *you* could be costing your business.

What you need
* An hourly rate for yourself.
* A timesheet.
* A way of accounting for your costs.

What you do
If you really want to know how your business is tracking and whether it's remotely profitable you need to include all the costs. And that includes a cost for *you*.

I don't care whether you pay yourself and what you pay yourself, but I do care about the effort that you are putting into your business for 'free'. The reason that I care and I desperately want *you* to care is that you could be making some poor decisions by excluding the 'you' factor.

For example, if you do all the labour in the manufacture of your stuff and you don't cost it, you may underprice your product. Or if you do all the admin and marketing and don't include this in your overheads, you may well think you are making a nice little profit but are really making a loss.

So here's what you do.

- Give yourself an hourly rate—maybe based on the annual salary you were getting out in the market, or on the amount you would need to pay someone to do the job that you are doing.
- Keep a timesheet—just a note each day of what you are spending your time on. Do this according to cost category—e.g. 2 hours on marketing, 3 hours on distribution.
- On a weekly or monthly basis, tally up the hours you have spent in each area and multiply this by your 'hourly rate' to get a cost.
- Each month, once you have printed off your reports from your accounting package, add the 'you' costs in (maybe in a spreadsheet) and see what the impact is.
- Think about adding the 'you' costs into your unit product cost.
- Now take a look at the result and ask yourself whether you are happy with how the business is tracking.

EverEscents

Leone Martin's interest in all things organic started after her grandmother was diagnosed with lymphatic cancer. The shattering news prompted Leone to start researching natural products and supplements that her grandmother could take to improve her wellbeing. Amazingly, her grandmother started to feel much better and went on to live eight years longer than her doctors predicted.

During her research Leone was horrified at the amount of chemicals found in ordinary shampoos, so she set about developing an organic range. Undeterred by her lack of experience, Leone threw herself into the project—devouring information on shampoos, chemicals and organic products, hiring cosmetic scientists to work on formulations and getting advice from world-class hairdressers. The result was the incredibly popular EverEscents Organic Hair Care range.

Leone had developed a great product, was terrific at marketing and she achieved the impossible: she sold product into hair salons that would normally turn their noses up at anything that wasn't an established brand.

But, as Leone herself says, the financial side of the business was an unwelcome challenge and not her forte. 'I just didn't really manage the costs,' she says, 'and one thing led to another. The costs were mounting and it was a stressful time. I took a second job so I could pay the suppliers of the business. I made a few mistakes I guess, got carried away investing in packaging and the like that seemed like a good deal at the time but in retrospect I couldn't afford.'

Leone was approached by a couple who wanted to buy the business. 'I originally said no. They gave me an offer that was hard to refuse and they asked me to think about it again. I stewed over it for a couple of weeks and then decided that I would be silly to hang on to it for sentimental reasons, so I sold. Along with the deal they offered me a position doing marketing (which is the part that I loved) and I no longer had to do the budgeting and accounting bit, which I really struggled with.'

Leone is no longer with EverEscents; instead she is putting her experience to good use as a business development consultant. But the company continues the practice that Leone started of donating 5 cents from every product sold to Camp Quality, a children's cancer charity.

Visit EverEscents at www.everescents.com.au.

Part III

CASH: YOUR BREAD AND BUTTER

Cash is the 'bread' of your business—the staple food, the life force—and the kitchen table tycoon rarely seems to have enough of it. It is an unfortunate fact of business that you can merrily be making a profit and come unstuck because you have no cash.

I know that sounds counter-intuitive, but it does happen. And mostly when it does, it's a nasty surprise. There are plenty of reasons for this unfortunate turn of events and, contrary to popular thought, it is often less to do with the relatively empty piggy bank your business starts with and more about managing stuff like recalcitrant debtors and an abundance of inventory.

It's actually not that fiddly to create a little more cash in your business. You just need a few tricks up your sleeve.

The first is about reducing the amount of time that elapses between when you buy stock and when you finally sell it. It's called your cash cycle. You don't need to get too technical about calculating it; you just need to know what it is so that you can shrink it. More on this in chapter 10.

The second trick is predicting your cash levels. It's not quite crystal balls and tarot cards; instead, it's a cash flow forecast. I find it a little more practical than channelling the spirits, although maybe not quite as fun. And because even the sound of the word 'forecast' can render some kitchen table tycoons quite fragile, chapter 11 provides a short collection of recipes for a no-fuss forecast.

I have not included any recipes here for borrowing money. That's not because I think there is anything wrong with borrowing money. I just think you should save your credit for when you need to finance something big and out of the ordinary (like a computer). For your day-to-day cash needs I urge you to try self-creation first. Baking your own bread is really quite uncomplicated and makes for a far better business.

Basic White Bread

This recipe is almost easier than ducking out to the shops!

WHAT YOU NEED

500 g strong white flour
1 tbsp salt
60 ml olive oil
20 g fresh yeast
270 ml water

WHAT YOU DO

Mix all the ingredients together in a large bowl. Knead well and leave in a draught-free place to rise for 1 hour. Form the dough into a sausage shape and place in an oiled 450 g loaf tin. Leave to rise for another hour. Preheat the oven to 230°C. Bake for 35 minutes, or until crusty and golden on top.

10

CASH CYCLE: THE BASIC WHITE BREAD RECIPES

*H*ealth zealots would have us believe that there is no place for white bread. I disagree. Sometimes the very thing that we need is effortless sustenance.

I feel rather the same way about accounting zealots who get overexcited in their creation of number-crunchingly nutritious ways to improve one's cash managment. The result is often something that's tough to pull together and a complete anathema to understand.

So I say bake the cash management equivalent of white bread. Create simple nourishment that is easy to put together and quick to digest. The business recipes in this chapter should do just that.

They start with a look at what is happening in your business right now by introducing you to your operating cycle and your cash cycle. These cycles sound far more complicated than they actually are. The operating cycle, quite simply, is the journey your stuff goes on from the moment you order the raw materials from the supplier through to delivery to your customer. Taking in, of course, its travels to the manufacturer, its trip to your garage, its repackaging and its lounging around waiting to be sold.

Once you and your operating cycle are best buddies, its spouse—the cash cycle—is a doddle to understand. The cash cycle is just the pottering about that your cash does while your stuff is travelling through the operating cycle. And it is the 'pottering' element that is so often the problem. It seems that cash can be rather inclined to make a speedy exit from your business but can be very lax and unfocused about actually coming home.

Following the recipes in this chapter should provide all the techniques you need to speed up your operating and cash cycles and create a bit more cash in your business. And because these recipes are so basic they are easily within the capabilities of even the most accounting-averse kitchen table tycoon.

Any time you are feeling a bit exasperated try making the Basic White Bread recipe on page 130. It's delicious of course, but the real magic is in the kneading. You can't beat a good pummelling!

Rising Your Dough

Don't feel you have to work through these recipes in order. There is absolutely no need to be on top of your operating and cash cycles before you become mistress of your cash and start wielding some discipline.

Yet the benefit of working through the 'cycle' recipes is that they give you a good idea of what is happening in your business right now and the particular areas that are ripe for tackling. It's amazing how a small amount of attention in the right place can garner a big improvement in your bank balance.

Another reason to try the 'cycle' recipes is that they will give you a wonderful sense of achievement. Do them now and see what your business looks like, then once you have given the techniques in the 'action' recipes some time to work, run through your cycles again. You will be able to see the fruits of your endeavours in black and white. What can be more motivating than that?

The cycle recipes:

❖ Getting to know your operating cycle.
❖ Getting to know your cash cycle.

The action recipes:

❖ Speeding up your operating cycle.
❖ Collecting cash more quickly.
❖ Spending cash more slowly.

These recipes are not about perfection. You don't need to tie yourself up in knots getting the exact measurements for your cash cycle. A rough idea will do. It's homemade bread after all—it's for eating, not looking at.

Getting to know your operating cycle

We are not very good at feeling the time. A big night out on the town can feel like an hour; the cold 15-minute wait for a taxi home can feel like forever.

You might be surprised by how long your operating cycle is.

What you need
❖ A picture of your operating cycle to see how long it takes.

What you do
The first thing to do is to draw a picture of how your business works. Start at the very beginning and go through the whole process. How do you buy your ingredients? How do you make your product? How do you store it? How do you sell it? How do you get paid for it?

Now put together the timings—how long does it take for your product to make its journey through all the phases? Let's say you have a biscuit business; the timing may look something like this.

Day 1—order flour, eggs, butter, sugar and cocoa powder.

Day 4—deliver ingredients to manufacturer.

Days 6 to 8—manufacture biscuits.

Day 9—deliver biscuits to refrigerated warehouse.

Day 10—staff repackage biscuits into smaller packs.

Days 11 to 40—distribute biscuits to customers.

So this is telling us that it takes between 11 and 40 days to complete one start-to-finish in your business. In other words, it takes 11 to 40 days to complete one operating cycle.

I think it's worth playing private detective on your business here. Instead of just writing down what you think the operating cycle times should be, delve into your business and actually calculate them. I am always amazed at how things take so much longer to do than I imagine.

Getting to know your cash cycle

A little business with a long cash cycle is little like a dachshund: it doesn't make sense.

If you are not a doggy person you may be unfamiliar with these sweet-natured little chaps with tiny legs, very long bodies, an over-enthusiasm for food and a propensity for prolapsed discs. But you might recognise the little business with a long cash cycle. It's the one with the amenable business owner who pays her suppliers quickly, gives her adored customers heaps of credit, has an over-enthusiasm for purchasing stock and gets stressed about cash.

Is your business a dachshund?

What you need

❖ To know what your cash cycle looks like.

❖ A simple spreadsheet.

❖ Access to your cash records.

What you do

Your cash cycle is simply the time that elapses between when you first pay your suppliers and when you finally collect cash from your customers.

Start by taking your operating cycle from the previous recipe and note down when your actual cash payments and receipts happen.

Continuing the example in the previous recipe, the cash cycle for your biscuit business may look a bit like this.

Day 1—you are a small business so the supplier demands cash on delivery. You pay for the ingredients in full.

Day 4—pay manufacturer a deposit of half the manufacturing cost.

Day 9—take delivery of the biscuits, they taste good. Pay the manufacturer the balance of the invoice, pay delivery man.

Day 10—pay employees for day's work.

Days 11 to 40—pay delivery man.

Day 41—first customer pays.

Day 100—last customer pays.

Next, in a spreadsheet, rustle up a table like the one below.

	Day	Cash (out)/in	Cash running total
Starting cash in the bank	0		$0
Ingredients	1	($70,000)	($70,000)
Manufacturing deposit	4	($25,000)	($95,000)
Manufacturing final payment	9	($25,000)	($120,000)
Delivery man payment	9	($1000)	($121,000)
Pay employees for packing	10	($1000)	($122,000)
Pay customer delivery man	Say daily from days 11 to 40	($3000)	($125,000)
First customer pays	41	$20,000	($105,000)
Other customers pay	Average (to make the example easier) 75	$110,000	$5000
Last customer pays	100	$20,000	$25,000

Then take a look at how the cash flows out of and into the business.

At first glance the biscuit business looks to be a no-brainer—after all it makes a profit of $25,000. But look at what happens to the cash. You would have to pay out $125,000 in real money in the first 40 days and not even get the initial cash back until around day 75.

Look for the points where your cash balance really drops and keep this in mind for the next recipes. These are the bits to focus on—the places where just a small change in your terms of trade can make a big difference to your hip pocket. And this is what is so liberating: instead of having a big worry about money generally, you can put all that energy to work on changing just a few specifics.

The examples in these recipes are deliberately simple. You will probably find that your cash flows vary quite a bit, so just take an average. Don't get too bogged down in accuracy.

Speeding up your operating cycle

Apparently it can take a woman up to one and a half hours to get ready for a night out compared to a man's 15 minutes. The reason for this, it seems, is the overwhelming number of options we have at our disposal when we get ready: I read somewhere that our choices extend to over 100 beauty items and more than 200 outfit combinations.

In a business, the more options, choices and stock lines you offer your customers, the more likely it is that you will have a long operating cycle. And that long operating cycle is costing you money.

What you need

❖ Your operating cycle from the earlier recipe.

❖ A little imagination.

What you do

To speed up your operating cycle, grab hold of the information you collected in the first recipe and look at where the big chunks of time are.

Most often you will find that time is swallowed up by mounds of raw materials (bought because they were cheap/available/volume-discounted) and mountains of finished goods (made because you had spare manufacturing time/like to hold a wide variety/got overexcited about demand).

Here are some suggestions to shorten your operating cycle and free up your cash.

❖ Narrow your product range.

❖ Buy raw materials only when you need them.

* Don't make stuff just because you can—make it because you have a customer.
* Encourage customers to place regular orders or order in advance so you can make to order.
* Sell your old stock—it is probably better to have the cash working in your business, even if it means selling the stock at a loss.

Try not to get too caught up in believing that your operations have to be conducted in a certain way. Spend a bit of time being imaginative and think about how you would *ideally* like to run the business.

Collecting cash more quickly

Kitchen table tycoons simply don't have the 'legs' to support a big bellyful of customers who dilly-dally about paying.

But sometimes customers don't even realise they are being recalcitrant. A friend recently went to pay her son's preschool fees and was astonished to learn that she hadn't paid for almost six months. She swears it wasn't intentional (she is a natural forget-a-lot) and says that in the 104 visits she made to the school since her previous payment (twice a day, five days a week for half a year) she had not had a single verbal reminder.

What you need
❖ Ten ways to compel your customers to pay more quickly.

What you do
Try these 10 suggestions for speeding up your cash collections.

1. DO YOUR HOMEWORK
If you can, run a credit check on new customers. You don't want to get fleeced. If you can't run a credit check, or they are a small business with no track record, ask for cash on delivery until they have proved themselves to be good customers.

2. DETAILS
It's a little thing but very important: make sure that your terms and conditions of sale are spelled out very clearly. Tell your customers over and over again what your terms of trade are so there can be no excuse for them 'not realising that your terms were seven days'.

3. DISCOUNTS
Think about giving customers a discount for paying quickly. If you are going to do this though you need to do three things:
❖ Check that you can afford to give the discount—how much is it going to eat into the profit you make on this sale?

❖ Only give the discount if the customer pays within the time period (say 10 days)—be tough or you will get a reputation for being a walkover.

❖ Weigh up which you need more: the cash or the profit.

4. DEPOSITS

Ask for a deposit before you send the goods, or ask for a part payment on delivery or even the full cash in advance. Think about how you can make this attractive to your customer. I once read about a pet-food shop that offered customers a significant discount when they paid for a year's food upfront. The shop stored it for free and the customers just dropped by when they needed it. This trick worked for everyone. The customers got a nice discount for buying in bulk and the pet shop was able to use the cash to negotiate both volume and speedy-payer discounts.

5. DIRECT DEBITS

For your regular customers, organise a monthly payment (like a magazine subscription). It will help your cash flow and may also help customer retention—and this is important as it's much cheaper to keep a customer than to find a new one. And make it easy for your customers to pay you, which means accepting credit cards. (Yes, I know credit card charges are high, but accept it as a cost of doing business: no credit card, no business.)

6. DIARISE

Unless all your sales are in cash, you will need to chase your debtors. Because this is not much fun most people avoid it like the plague. This is great news for customers, because if you don't hassle them they won't worry about paying you. As it's not a job you want to do, I suggest that you make a regular time in your diary for doing it. This gets it over and done with once a week and then you don't need to think about it again. First thing in the morning is a good time, and early in the week so you can get your invoice settled in their end-of-week cheque run.

7. DEBTOR DANCING

This is about making friends with the guy in your customer's payment department. You've got to feel sorry for him: day in, day out he's taking calls from suppliers demanding cash with menaces, and all the while his boss is breathing down his neck telling him not to pay anyone. You need to charm him a bit and get him to like you so that he processes *your* payment before anyone else's!

8. DAILY

Okay, so debtor dancing didn't work. Now you need to get persistent and call every day. Sooner or later they will get fed up and pay you just so that you go away.

9. DEBT FACTORING AND INVOICE DISCOUNTING

These are official things. Debt factoring is where you sell your invoices to a debt-factoring company. They give you cash in advance and for that they take your invoices and collect the cash. Obviously the cash they give you is substantially smaller than the total of your invoices. But sometimes cash is more important than profit.

Invoice discounting is similar in that the invoice discounter gives you a cash advance on the basis of your debtors, but you still have the responsibility for collecting the cash. So you chase the debtors and repay the invoice discounter. Again the charges for this service are quite considerable.

These services may not suit you or you may not be eligible for them, but it's handy to know they exist.

10. DEBT COLLECTORS

When is it time to bring in the heavies? Debt collectors and legal proceedings are a last resort, but if someone really won't pay it may be your only course of action. It is expensive though and you may find that the legal costs outweigh your debt. Sometimes, painful as it is, you just have to walk away.

The bottom line is that many customers will always take ages to pay, but don't let them. You need the money more than they do.

Spending cash more slowly

I'm not suggesting anything improper here and I certainly don't subscribe to the idea that you should make life tougher for another business. No, I am simply wanting you to feel empowered to take that which is rightfully yours.

What you need
⟡ Eight ways to decelerate your creditor payments.

What you do
Try the ideas below.

1. CREDIT HISTORY
One of the problems of being a new business is that you don't have a track record and suppliers may be a bit nervous about dealing with you so they ask you to pay in advance. You can't create a credit history from nothing, but one thing you can do is to create your own history with your regular suppliers. Tell them that you will pay them in advance the first two times, then you will take a 10-day credit period (and stick to it!) and slowly extend it. Every time you must meet your commitments on time, or you will be back to square one.

2. CONFIDENCE

Act like a sizeable business and be confident with your suppliers. Challenge them about their payment terms. Big businesses are shocking at paying bills and some of them take enormous credit periods.

3. CHECK CONDITIONS

Before you sign up with a supplier, review their terms and conditions carefully and discuss them. You need to be clear about the payment expectations and then manage them, not just put your head in the sand and hope they go away!

4. CREATIVITY

Be innovative and creative about your supplier arrangements. What would work better for you? Can you ask a supplier to sell you stock on a consignment basis (where you only pay for what you sell)?

5. CHAT

Talk to your supplier. They want your business, so join forces and work together to find a way of managing the cash flow that will work for both of you.

6. CHEQUE RUN

Have a weekly cheque run and only process payments on that day. Tell your suppliers that you will pay them on Friday—it gives you a few extra days to pay, plus it is far more time efficient to do all your payments at once.

7. CRACK DOWN ON DISCOUNTS

Discounts sound great but if you are short of cash, don't be sucked in by promises of savings. There are two types of discounts that may look appealing, but need careful consideration.

1. Early-bird discounts—although these will save you costs, if you are strapped for cash you may want to take the extra few weeks' credit instead.
2. Big-bird (bulk) discounts—volume discounts are great if you really need that volume, but otherwise you will have a bigger cash outlay than you can afford and the stuff will just end up sweating away in a warehouse.

8. CHOOSE YOUR SUPPLIERS

Look at who you work with and who can afford to extend you a bit more credit. If you are doing a lot of work with a small business they probably can't afford to help you out, but a larger one can. If you know things are going to be a bit tight, see if you can negotiate a payment plan.

Anasazi

When Margaret Butler started her homewares business, Anasazi, she used her credit card to finance the first purchase of inventory. She decided then and there that it would be the only borrowing the business would do. Margaret inherited her parents' 'no borrowing' philosophy and, although it looked impossible, she was determined to finance the company through cash flow.

Essentially Anasazi sources homeware products which it sells into major retailers, a process that usually requires significant working capital to manage the time lag between paying for purchases and receiving cash from sales.

To manage without borrowing, Margaret understood the need for a short operating and cash cycle. As she explains: 'I have always had a very tight range of customers and products and I am obsessive about selling only great products—the big demand for product is a great negotiating tool when it comes to collecting cash. I also made sure my business formula worked before I expanded—sometimes businesses think that they can expand themselves out of trouble, but in my experience if you do that you just grow a bigger problem.'

Margaret is very creative, but has always seen the need to be on top of the numbers. 'Knowing that I have got a good formula for my business makes space for me to pursue the creative side. Although I will admit that it took me longer than it probably should have to realise that the key to running a good business is to use my hands less and my brain more.'

To say that Margaret exudes enthusiasm for her business just doesn't do her justice. It is undoubtedly one of the reasons behind her enormous success, but it is her attitude that 'small business doesn't need to get kicked around' that has proved a real winner. And she has shown how a little cash can go a long, long way.

Visit Anasazi at www.anasazihome.com.

Tea Bread

This is my grandmother's recipe and it is simply delicious.

WHAT YOU NEED

300 ml cold tea

115 g soft dark brown sugar

200 g mixed dried fruit

1 tbsp honey

1 egg, beaten

285 g self-raising flour

½ tsp ginger

WHAT YOU DO

Mix the tea, sugar, dried fruit and honey in a bowl and allow to soak overnight.

Preheat the oven to 160°C and line a small loaf tin with greaseproof paper. Add the beaten egg, flour and ginger to the fruit mixture. Bake for 1 hour 10 minutes. Best when still a little sticky in the middle.

11

CASH FLOW FORECAST: THE TEA BREAD RECIPES

*I*f you have decided a cash flow forecast is simply out of the question, I am not entirely surprised. At first blush it looks off-puttingly complicated and desperately time consuming. Why would you want to spend your precious time making predictions when you could be spending it making sales?

However, because I have seen cash flow surprises unravel many little businesses I feel almost dictatorial in my desire for you to have a basic idea of the ebbs and flows of money in your business. So I am not going to capitulate and agree that a cash flow forecast is not worth the bother, but will instead suggest that you can get away with a quick version rather than the laborious real thing.

This chapter, then, is dedicated to the fuss-free Tea Bread version of the cash flow forecast.

Tea bread is a quick fruit bread—the time-poor cook's answer to the real thing. Now, just because it is quick doesn't mean it is any less delicious: yes, it tastes different to the conventional fruit loaf, but is scrumptious in its own right.

The same can be said for the quick cash flow technique in this chapter. It is not designed to be held up as a great example of a cash flow forecast, but to give you a third alternative to the usual heads-you-do-it-properly, tails-you-don't-do-it-at-all option. It will help you predict your big cash flows, which I think is what really matters.

Is quick bread cheating? I don't think so. If you are in any doubt, try the Tea Bread recipe on page 150. My grandmother would read the tea leaves before she made the bread—can you?

CASH FLOW: READING THE TEA LEAVES

This cash flow technique is designed to fit into the busy life you lead. Rather than spend ages finessing your spreadsheet skills and perfecting your estimates of the timing of payments, this is just a quick way to get an idea of the way cash flows in your business.

Much like the financial food processor in chapter 5, the quick cash flow is actually a workbook of four interconnecting spreadsheets. And if you worked through that chapter you will glide through this one. If you haven't done the financial food processor and are consumed with anxiety about spreadsheets, please don't be. These recipes are very simple, so relax and remember that spreadsheets are just a tool (a bit like a bread machine): it's the ingredients you put into it that are important.

I estimate my cash flows by month because I think it gives just enough of a guide to the ebbs and flows, without having to go overboard on detail.

The four spreadsheets are pages for four different types of data.

- Spreadsheet 1 is called 'Summary cash flow' and it just shows two things: your net cash movement for the month, and your closing cash balance.
- Spreadsheet 2 is called 'Detailed cash flows' and shows, line by line, all the cash inflows and outflows for the month.
- Spreadsheet 3 is called 'Estimates—sales and costs'.
- Spreadsheet 4 is called 'Workings—receipts and payments'.

Remember, a simple cash flow model that gives a good indication of cash flows is better than a complicated, intricate model that tries to be massively accurate but loses it somewhere in the formulas. So the point is to get started. It won't be perfect, but that doesn't matter. Something is better than nothing.

Spreadsheet 1: summary cash flow

There is nothing quite like a malnourished cash flow forecast to galvanise you into action. And it's so much less panic-inducing when you actually have a bit of time to do something about it.

What you need
❖ A spreadsheet that summarises your forecast net cash movement.

What you do
A simple start to ease you in gently—just set up a spreadsheet like the one below (no numbers yet, and just a couple of formulas).

Month	January	February	March
Opening cash	(a)	(b)	
Net movement in month	(c)		
Closing cash	(b)		

(a) Starting point

(b) Next month's opening balance is last month's closing balance

(c) From 'Detailed cash flows'

As this is a quick cash flow, you can use your bank balance as the starting point. If you want to be more accurate, use your cash book balance (see The Pantry).

Spreadsheet 2: detailed cash flows

This spreadsheet really just expands on the previous one. I like to keep them separate so that the summary on spreadsheet 1 is nicely uncluttered; too many lines and I get distracted.

What you need
❖ A list of the important categories of cash inflows and outflows—just whatever makes sense to you.

What you do
Set up a detailed spreadsheet that looks something like the one on page 156. You want to have a line dedicated to each category of inflow and outflow.

This spreadsheet mainly just pulls numbers from spreadsheet 4. The most complicated bit will be adding a few categories of costs together to get a total for overheads.

Month	January	February	March
Cash inflows:			
Sales			
Total cash inflows			
Cash outflows:			
Purchases			
Salaries			
Overheads			
Total cash outflows			
Net change in cash (cash inflows less cash outflows)			

Spreadsheet 3: estimates—sales and costs

Before you can even contemplate the timing of your cash payments and receipts you will need to have some idea of what your sales and costs will actually be. This is fun; not only is it the making-it-up bit, but also, if you have worked through the earlier chapters, you have already done the hard work. Phew.

What you need
-※- Your budget.

What you do

Joy of joys, the estimate of your actual sales and costs is just your budget for the year ahead. If you have done one already, then go and get it; if not, flick back to the second recipe in chapter 9, 'Budget your costs for the year ahead'.

I suggest that you start by simply copying your budget into this spreadsheet, calling the budget column 'total budget'. Then set up an additional 12 columns—one for each month. Like this:

Month	Total budget	January	February	March
Sales:				
Sales—product line 1				
Sales—product line 2				
Total sales				
Costs:				
Stock purchases				
Salaries				
Rent				
Insurance				
Net profit				

Now, for each cost line in your 'total budget' column you will need to make an educated guess as to which month or months you will receive the purchase invoices. This will probably be very easy for costs such as overheads but a bit trickier for your purchases of stock—just do your best; it won't be perfect but it will get easier with a bit of practice. You want to end up with your budgeted costs spread across the 12 monthly columns.

You will also need to spread your budgeted sales across the 12 months. Try to avoid apportioning your sales equally across the months; instead think about the busy and quiet times of your business (e.g. how will the summer holidays impact you?) and also bear in mind that if your business is growing, you would expect your monthly sales to grow towards the end of the year too.

Spreadsheet 4: workings—
receipts and payments

I have to say that this is the trickiest part of the cash flow forecast. But if you take it step by step, I promise you it really is just common sense.

What you need
- ❖ Your cash cycle from the recipe 'Getting to know your cash cycle' in chapter 10.

What you do

First of all you will need to set up another spreadsheet identical to spreadsheet 3, 'Estimates—sales and costs', but without the numbers in it. Then you need to grab your cash cycle and remind yourself how long it takes your debtors to pay, and how quickly you pay your suppliers.

Then, starting with sales, take the monthly entries in spreadsheet 3 and ask yourself when you will receive the cash. Try to come up with a formula for this: for example, if you receive the cash for half of your sales in the month of invoicing and half in the month following, then your formula for February will be: ½ × January sales + ½ × February sales.

Do exactly the same for your costs: simply work across the monthly entries in spreadsheet 3 and ask yourself 'When will we pay this?', and pop the formula into the appropriate cell in the spreadsheet on page 160.

Once you have done this have a think about whether you are likely to make any payments that aren't in your budget—such as asset purchases or tax—and then add a couple of lines to your spreadsheet to include these too.

I also think it's useful to jot down on the spreadsheet the assumptions you have made about the timing of receipts and payments. Every so often, check that you are happy with these assumptions and, if you are not, simply change the formulas in the spreadsheet to reflect real life!

Month	January	February	March
Sales: cash receipts			
Receipts—product line 1	Formula	Formula	Formula
Receipts—product line 2	Formula	Formula	Formula
Total cash inflow			
Costs: payments			
Stock payments	Formula	Formula	Formula
Salary payments	Formula	Formula	Formula
Rent payments	Formula	Formula	Formula
Insurance payments	Formula	Formula	Formula
Total cash outflow			

It's always tricky to find a neat starting point with your cash flow, and when you actually do this spreadsheet you will see that January (or whichever month you picked as your first) looks a bit empty. That is because January is likely to be the month where the cash flows fall relating to sales and purchases that occurred before the start of your budget. So I suggest you give a bit of extra thought to the receipts and payments in your opening months.

Finally, my advice is to just get on and have a go; the formulas won't be hard if you think about it logically and don't try to get too complicated. Remember, this is quick bread, not perfect bread.

quick bites

A note about tax: there are some quirky things about tax that you may need to include in your cash flow. If you are feeling a little puzzled about when and how you pay tax, give your accountant, or the tax office, a quick call.

GETTING THE BEST OUT OF YOUR CASH FLOW

To make the best use of your cash flow forecast, compare your actual cash flows with your forecast ones, try to understand the difference and, if necessary, make amendments to your assumptions. I also suggest that you update your cash flow at the start of every month for your actual opening cash.

ANOTHER REASON TO DO A CASH FLOW

If you are feeling a little disinclined to do a cash flow forecast, here is another little benefit. By playing around with the assumptions in spreadsheet 4 you will be able to see how a small change in your cash cycle can make a big impact on your cash balance.

WeeWunz

When Nicole Mills and Sheila Ghosh realised that the wait for childcare places would be longer than their maternity leave they decided to take action. They didn't, as you might think, open a childcare centre; instead they embarked on a somewhat grander scheme to provide businesses with childcare solutions for their employees. The business has been so successful that it has now broadened its services into solutions for the care of elderly family members.

A growing business eats cash. A consulting business eats cash. Put them both together and you have no choice but to be on top of your cash flow forecast game.

Says Nicole, 'Our business is a consulting business; we sell the know-how of our team. The trouble is that you can't stall payments to employees in the way that you may slow down payments to suppliers when cash gets tight, so we have to manage it very carefully.

We also work with large companies who can be frustratingly slow payers.'

Nicole and Sheila manage their business tightly and have had positive cash flows from day one.

As Nicole points out, 'If we hadn't been managing our cash flow we would never have been able to afford to grow our business.' And working families are happy they did: WeeWunz has been instrumental in helping companies provide much-needed child care for their hard-working employees.

Visit WeeWunz at www.weewunz.com.

Part IV

TIME: HAVING YOUR CAKE AND EATING IT TOO

I don't think anyone feels they have enough time to do their business justice.

For the kitchen table tycoon who starts her business as a lifestyle choice to fit work around her family this can be very frustrating. For the kitchen table tycoon who starts her business to change a small corner of the world it is maddening. For all of us, at one time or another, it can induce sheer panic. There is simply too much to do and not enough hours in the day to do it.

Sad to say, it's not uncommon for kitchen table tycoons to bin their business because they simply don't make enough money to justify all the hours they spend on it. Frustrated by an inability to increase profit, they give up—which is a shame, because they could try looking to make it work by reducing the time involved instead.

So, this section suggests ways to help you create what I call more 'people hours' for your business. This isn't about offloading your children onto your neighbour so you can spend more time working, or slaving away into the wee hours. It is about taking the 'people hours' that you already have and either getting more done with them or cleverly finding a few more.

The next chapter looks at ways to get through your jobs more quickly. I am not talking about adopting machine-like efficiency in everything you do, but rather being focused on what you are doing and why you are doing it. Often it's more about avoiding distractions than doing anything particularly revolutionary.

If you can't create more people hours, how about changing your business to reduce the number of people hours it needs? Sounds like wishful thinking I know, but actually a few painless modifications to the way you do things could free up some time. This is about changing the way you organise your business—more on this in chapter 13.

The final chapter in this section is about creating a few more people hours by actually buying some. It's the business equivalent of hiring a kitchen hand, seeking advice from a top chef or outsourcing production to a factory. Though frequently considered a luxury, it is often the best money you will ever spend, and the business recipes in that chapter will help you spend your money wisely.

Chocolate Cake

Very, very chocolatey

WHAT YOU NEED
250 g butter
300 g light muscovado sugar
5 eggs
300 g dark chocolate, melted
100 g plain flour
100 g self-raising flour

WHAT YOU DO
Preheat the oven to 160°C and line a 20 cm cake tin. In a saucepan, melt the chocolate and allow to cool a little. Beat the butter and sugar together in a large bowl until light and creamy. Beat in the eggs one at a time, then the melted chocolate. Fold in the flour.

Pour the batter into the cake tin and bake for 1½ hours. Leave to cool, then ice lavishly, or sprinkle with icing sugar.

12

FREE YOURSELF UP: THE CHOCOLATE BIRTHDAY CAKE RECIPES

I remember being consumed with jaw-dropping envy when I first encountered a homemade Fairy Princess birthday cake at a two-year-old's birthday party. When the same Fairy Princess cake turned up at every subsequent party I started to feel enormous discomfort. Either I had stumbled upon a group of mums who were undercover chefs, or this was a staple in the cake repertoire of the everyday mother. While by virtue of having a son I clearly wasn't expected to rustle up a Fairy Princess, his birthday was next and a simple sponge, I realised, just wasn't going to pass muster.

Then I discovered the secret of impossibly easy children's birthday cakes: a cookbook laden with step-by-step pictures, copious instructions, shopping lists and detailed planning to make the process quick and effortless for even the most disorganised cook. The result: a birthday cake that was stunning to look at and speedy to do.

So if your business has an insatiable appetite for your time, use some of the following techniques to make yourself a bit more effective. By this I don't mean turning yourself into one of those frighteningly capable people who get things done at the speed of light; rather I mean doing things purposefully—doing the important stuff first, and being organised.

While this just sounds like commonsense I don't think that many of us, and I include myself here, actually do it. In fact, sitting down to write these recipes gave me my own personal prod in the ribs. I needed it; I am a master at getting gloriously distracted.

So these little tricks are to help you create more of your own time without just working longer. They are designed to help you be more efficient in a whole baking-a-business way, meaning that instead of just ploughing through the jobs on your to-do list you focus on the stuff that will make your business better, not the stuff that will just make your list shorter.

Of course, not having enough time is a wonderful excuse for simply not doing the jobs that you don't want to do. So if at first you're feeling a little reluctant to forge ahead, just bake up the delicious Chocolate Birthday Cake and treat yourself for starters.

FREE UP SOME TIME IN A SNAP

These recipes require absolutely no expertise and very little in the way of preparation.

The first three are quite intuitive and are really a reminder of the basics; they will help you focus your mind and bulldoze through the clutter. The fourth recipe—the timesheet one—is always a real eye-opener and will have you making better decisions about what you do and don't do. The final recipe is about using mentors, coaches and advisory boards—the equivalent of having Nigella Lawson on the phone once a month—to give you a few tips on how to change the way you bake to give a better result.

The five quick recipes are:

- Goals.
- Planning.
- Focus.
- Timesheets.
- Owls.

This isn't about taking the adrenaline and excitement out of your business, but simply about putting in fewer hours.

Goals

Being burstingly busy is so very on-trend. Who needs to worry about the fickleness of fashion when it is your *busyness* that is so de rigueur?

I know from first-hand experience how easy and enticing it is to be just 'too busy darling' when in fact you are actually just running around zealously achieving nothing.

If you would rather be a little less busy and a little more purposeful, indulge yourself in some goals.

What you need
❖ Goals.

What you do
Create a nest of goals; something akin to stackable mixing bowls or a set of Russian matryoshka dolls. You will need a massive one, a big one, a middling one, a little one and a tiny one which all fit snugly together.

MASSIVE GOALS
You need to have some really big goals for your business and I've pretty well covered that in chapter 2. Keep these pinned up on the wall in front of you to remind you of what this is all about.

A massive goal might be to have 50 shops in five years.

BIG GOALS

Set some big goals for the year ahead. These are a bit easier to focus on than massive goals, but are not as juicy. When you have set your big goals you need to work on your game plan for achieving those goals (see chapters 3 and 4).

A big goal might be to open three shops in the next year.

MIDDLING GOALS

I like to break my big goals into a series of middling goals, which are things to achieve in the next 100 days. Middling goals are ambitious but achievable.

A middling goal might be to open the first shop in the next 100 days.

LITTLE GOALS

You can then break the middling goals of 100 days into bite-sized goals of 10 days. This helps you to easily see what you need to accomplish in the next 10 days to keep you on track for your 100-day goal.

A little goal may be to get the interior of the shop painted.

TINY GOALS

This is simply the goal for the day ahead and is covered in the third recipe in this chapter, 'Focus'.

Your tiny goal may be to draw up the invite list for the store opening.

And that's it really: a little nest of goals all fitting tidily together and keeping you on track.

Planning

Years ago, when I was single and hoping that my horoscope would predict an imminent boyfriend, I read an article about the Aries woman, describing us as impulsive and impatient. I quite liked this because, even though it was intended as an insult, it gave me all the latitude I needed to continue to dive headlong into projects without bothering with anything so boring as planning.

Many moons later, while I would like to congratulate myself on camouflaging my no-plan style, I have to be honest and admit that I spent much of that time lurking down blind alleys and wasting time.

What you need
- ❖ Time to plan.
- ❖ Goals.
- ❖ A sprinkling of tactics.

What you do

Hard as it is, you need to set aside a little bit of thinking time for planning. Book it into your diary as you would an important client meeting and be as fastidious in keeping to it.

If you have followed the previous recipe you will now be armed with your goals and ready to discuss tactics. I realise that tactics have a terribly military sound to them but they are really just the 'how you are going to do it'. And of course what we are looking for is the quickest and most expedient way of doing the 'how'.

If you have hit a brick wall and can't figure out the best way of doing the 'how', enlist the help of your Owls (see the last recipe in this chapter).

quick bites

Do you ever get that overwhelming and sudden urge to do something that you really didn't plan on doing? I do and I am a firm believer in listening to and acting on gut feelings.

But doesn't this fly in the face of planning? Not at all. Planning is for the innumerable times when we need a map to get to our destination. Gut feelings just happen. And isn't it great that they do!

Focus

The ludicrous thing about being a magnificent multi-tasker is that it makes uni-tasking despairingly uncomfortable. Have you noticed how impossible it is to settle into the task at hand without fidgeting around doing a few other bits on the side?

I think as women we have done ourselves a bit of a disservice with this multi-tasking lark. I have become adept at '10 jobs done concurrently but not quite properly' and hopeless at getting the one really important brain-hurting piece done.

Definitely time to pamper ourselves with single-minded focus.

What you need

- New habits.
- Awareness of your best times and worst times.
- Daily goals.

What you do

- Preheat your mind by tolerating the fact that it takes three long weeks to form a new habit.
- Understand your best and worst times. Are you a morning person or a night owl? When do you find it easiest to focus and be your best? Uni-task when you are at your best and multi-task when you are feeling a bit lacklustre.

- Set daily goals at the end of every day. Yes, set them tonight for tomorrow. It feels good and it works.
- Diarise time to spend on important stuff.
- Turn off your phone, email and BlackBerry.

Being focused is about concentrating your attention; sounds easy but it's actually the hardest job for some of us.

And then there is always so much to do that it is temptingly easy to relegate the brain-ache and unpleasant things (cold-calling new customers, working out next year's strategy, chasing debtors) to the back seat so that you can busily tick off effortless stuff like popping to the post office. Beware the manically-busy-accomplishing-nothing cloak.

Concentrating on hard stuff is difficult, so give yourself plenty of breaks and make the total time quite short.

The point about focus is that you don't do it all day every day, so don't feel guilty about enjoying your easy tasks, and don't forget to take a bit of time to completely relax. You will be all the better for it.

Timesheets

The key to thriftiness is, I think, about being able to measure the success of your virtue. So if you are being frugal in the cash department, you can quite easily measure what you have saved and bathe in the warm glow of accomplishment.

But when you are striving to be so economical with your time it can feel a bit pointless: after all, if spending it is inevitable, why worry about doing it sparingly?

This recipe delights in turning your time into something you can taste.

What you need
❖ An hourly rate.
❖ A diary or timesheet.

What you do
Time is priceless, but you need to start giving it an hourly cost. Not a real cost (too hard to work out), but a pretend cost flavoured with a dash of reality.

A nice and simple way to do this is to base it on what you could be earning back in 'employment land'. If that is an annual salary, simply divide it by the rough number of hours you would have been working per year in that job (remembering to deduct long-forgotten niceties like annual leave).

Next step is to create a sort of timesheet. You can do this in a diary, but the quickest way is to set up a spreadsheet that looks something like this.

Task	Hours	Cost
		Formula (hours × hourly cost)

Every day, simply record in your timesheet everything that you have been working on and the number of hours it took. The spreadsheet will then calculate the cost of your time.

This is really no different to keeping a daily food diary if you are trying to lose weight. The food diary works by getting you to list, on a daily basis, everything that you eat. Once you have written all your little treats down in black and white it is hard to avoid the fact that your expanding girth is rather more to do with Genoa cake than genetics.

The same thing happens here: within a few days of starting your timesheet you will begin to see a pattern emerge of where your time is going. And even if you are the most rabid detester of timesheets I am confident that you will find something illuminating in this process.

This timesheet stuff only works if you are nauseatingly honest with yourself. I have a friend who keeps a faux food diary which she only updates on lettuce-leaf days!

Take a good look at where you are spending your time and ask yourself, 'Is it worth it?' Give it a bit of thought because the answers aren't always obvious. You may have spent $1000 in time chasing down a customer to return a paltry $100 profit—at first blush this looks like a complete waste of time, but if the customer is going to serve as a great launching pad to get further business it may be a good investment.

Owls

One of the absolute delights of having your own business is being boss-less. Until, that is, the novelty wears off and you find yourself wandering about aimlessly. Time for an injection of accountability.

What you need

A person who is happy to work with you for a couple of hours a month and who:

- has experience that is useful to you
- commands your respect
- you click with
- you don't want to let down
- you want to be held accountable to.

What you do

Much is made of the difference between mentors, coaches and chairmen. Don't get bogged down with it—you don't need a cast of thousands helping you, just someone who can save you from making mistakes, reinventing the wheel and dithering about aimlessly. To avoid any confusion I'm just going to call them Owls.

Finding an Owl is the first challenge so I suggest you draw up a picture of what you would like your Owl to 'look' like—what sort of experience you would like them to have, for instance—and then ask friends and family if they know anyone who fits the bill.

Once you have found a potential Owl, encourage them to want to help you by:

- explaining clearly how you think they can help (nothing worse than not really understanding what someone is asking you for)
- promising to keep their commitment small (maybe an hour once a month)
- saying that you are happy to get their advice by phone/email if they can't do 'in person' (phew)
- keeping them in touch with the business through weekly update emails (nice touch)
- being organised and professional—emailing them monthly discussion points a few days before the catch-up (give them a chance to find the nuggets).

At the monthly meeting:

* have a standing agenda—it's very reassuring to know what you are going to talk about
* prepare in advance—you don't want to waste a minute of your power hour
* send important info through to your Owl a few days before the meeting—but keep it brief
* take control of the meeting—it's not a chat fest.

Things that you might want to cover are:

* how the last month has gone (hard facts like numbers are good)
* progress against your goals
* what's going well and what's not
* your goals for the month ahead.

And you will know if the relationship is working if you feel that your Owl is:

* supporting you in tough decisions
* using their networks to support your business
* advocating for you
* warning you of crocodiles and keeping you out of trouble.

If you aren't getting benefit from your Owl, tactfully and speedily find a replacement.

quick bites

I know a kitchen table tycoon who also uses her Owl in a mythical capacity. Melissa is not very good at saying no to people, so if she gets herself into a pickle she says: 'I have discussed it with my chairman and he says we should decline on the basis of . . . and I agree with him.' He has probably said nothing of the sort—he may not even know the issue exists—but it allows her to play 'good cop' to a pretend 'bad cop'.

Angelic Events & Design

Jessica Eckford had a good corporate job but it wasn't satisfying her; what she really wanted to do was run an event-design company. So for a few years she did both. 'I set up Angelic Events & Design but for the first couple of years did it as a weekend job. In its early days the business couldn't afford to support me so I supported it by having a "proper job" too.'

Growing a business and working full-time is hard work, and I am not for one moment suggesting with this story that you should make more time by taking on another job. Rather, I'm making the point that working two jobs forces you into incredible efficiency, which is how Jessica pulled it off. 'I simply didn't have the time to muck around. Initially my goal was to grow the business to a point where I could work in it full-time. To make it happen I divided my goal into smaller goals, such as delivering a certain number of events in a three-month period, filling the order book for the upcoming wedding season, etc. It worked.'

From the moment she was in the business full-time, Angelic Events & Design has outperformed Jessica's expectations—and it's clear why. Jessica is tenacious, organised and focused. And she plans, plans, plans. That's not to say that she doesn't do things quickly and nimbly—she does—but she also makes the effort to consider the best way of doing things. And she doesn't get distracted; she knows the value of her time.

This shouldn't be a great surprise. After all, events put on by Angelic Events & Design are fastidiously well organised. But like the chiropodist with bunions, it's easy to be organised and planned for your customers, but much harder to be disciplined about yourself.

Visit Jessica at www.angelicevents.com.au.

Cupcakes

A lighter chocolate; well, that's my excuse for adding another chocolate cake recipe. But feel free to leave the cocoa powder out.

WHAT YOU NEED

110 g butter

110 g caster sugar

2 eggs

110 g self-raising flour

30 g cocoa powder

WHAT YOU DO

Preheat the oven to 180°C. Cream the butter and the sugar together until light and fluffy. Beat in the eggs. Fold in the flour and cocoa powder and spoon the batter into papercases in a muffin tin. Cook for 10–12 minutes, or until springy to touch.

Allow to cool, then decorate with chocolate icing. Makes 12.

13

FREE UP YOUR BUSINESS: THE CUPCAKE RECIPES

*F*unnily enough, cupcakes were invented as a kind of time-saver. Two hundred years ago someone who was clearly sick of cleaning up cake debris came up with the idea of giving children individually wrapped mini cakes to save on mess. I can't help but find it amusing then that I rediscovered cupcakes by eating the remnants discarded by my children.

Of course, mess is an enormous time waster and small businesses seem to get more than their fair share of it. Not in terms of crumbs and crumpled papercases but rather in mistakes, in reinventing what's already been done, and in quite simply losing things.

It's a vicious circle: lack of time leads to doing things hastily, haste leads to mistakes, mistakes lead to rework and rework takes time to do. Descent into abject confusion is hardly surprising.

But there is a solution to the mess problem and it comes in the guise of a sprinkling of processes. Now I do realise that this P-word conjures up pictures of bureaucracy and documents-in-triplicate but it doesn't have to be that bad. It's really just a standard way of doing things (where *you* pick the standard) and sticking to it.

The business recipes in this chapter are designed to help you look at the processes inside your business and give them a small tweak. And while I confess they take a little time to do, it's a case of what you spend in time now you get back in spades later.

Good processes are enormously comforting. It feels great to be confident that you can process things quickly and make few mistakes.

But if you really want comfort you can't go past a plate of real cupcakes, still warm from the oven. And, paradoxically, even when they are randomly decorated and arranged lazily on a plate they somehow seem beautifully organised.

GETTING YOUR PROCESSES DOWN PAT

Just because I implore you to adopt the P-word and have a standard way of doing things doesn't mean that I want you to stop experimenting. On the contrary, these recipes, which start by looking at your current processes, are designed to get you thinking about exploring new time-saving techniques.

Of course the greatest labour-saver is equipment: if you have ever beaten cake batter by hand you will appreciate the effort-reducing properties of the electric mixer. But you will see that I have not included any recipes for technology here. Clearly technology will, at some point, play an important part in your business; maybe it already does. But technology is a personal choice which is dependent on your type of business and size of wallet. So no technology recipes, just a couple of thoughts. The first is that you can make significant improvements to your processes without going on a technology shopping spree. Secondly, technology rarely solves the problems of human error and forgetfulness; it just sometimes hides them for a little while.

So here's what you need to do.

- Document your current processes.
- Look at how you can make them better.
- Ask yourself, 'What new processes do I need?'

Processes give you freedom. Unshackled by the demands of having to remember and rethink the day-to-day stuff, you get to concentrate instead on the more enjoyable bits of your business. But best of all, the P-word means that you can hand over your business to a stand-in for a couple of weeks while you take a holiday. Now, doesn't that sound good?

Document your current processes

This is the easiest of the three recipes, but because it's so simple the temptation is to skip over this recipe and get straight on with the next one. And, having done exactly that plenty of times, I can tell you it doesn't work.

So just enjoy the simplicity, grab a coffee and make a little bit of time to do this one.

What you need
* A clear mind.
* A couple of hours.

What you do
This recipe is simply about documenting your current processes. To do this just imagine you are going away on holiday and leaving a friend in charge of the business. Write her a series of instructions. If you are thinking that you don't have any processes, remember that they are just your 'usual way of doing things'.

To help you do this, think about your business in terms of three main processes: buying, doing and selling.

The **buying** process is all the steps you take, starting with ordering goods, through receiving them, to paying for them.

The **doing** process is simply all the steps you take to make your stuff, or if you are in a service business, all the steps you take to deliver your service. (By that I mean if you are a personal trainer, the way you run your sessions.)

The **selling** process is simply all the steps starting with taking a sales order, through dispatching it, to collecting the cash.

Now write down all the steps that your friend will need to do in order to buy, do or sell. Flick through the following checklists for a few examples of questions to help you document your buying and selling processes.

And that's it—until the next recipe, where you give your processes a jolly good overhaul.

For more inspiration, visit www.thebusinessbakery.com.au.

QUESTIONS TO HELP YOU DOCUMENT YOUR BUYING PROCESS

- How do you decide how much to order?
- How do you do your ordering?
- How do you check you are getting the best price?
- How often do you order? Is there a regular pattern?
- When goods are received, how do you check they are all there and in good condition?
- Do you check the quantities received against the invoice?

- Do you match the goods received note to the invoice?
- Do you write on the invoice that you have checked the goods received?
- Where and how do you file your unpaid invoices?
- When do you enter the invoice into your accounting system?
- How do you store your goods? (That is, inventory.)
- How do you keep the inventory in good shape?
- How do you organise the inventory?
- How do you know how old some of your inventory is?
- How often do you pay invoices?
- How do you decide when an invoice should be paid?
- How do you enter the payment into your accounting system?

QUESTIONS TO HELP YOU DOCUMENT YOUR SELLING PROCESS

- How does someone place an order?
- How do you check you can fulfil it?
- How do you know how to price it?
- How do you prepare the invoice?
- When do you send the invoice out?
- How do you dispatch it?
- How do you check that you don't send the order out twice?
- How do you confirm the product was received?
- Do you print out a copy of the customer invoice and file it as unpaid?

- How do you enter the invoice in your accounting records?
- How often do you chase invoice payment?
- What do you do with recalcitrant debtors?
- How do you bank the cash?
- How do you reconcile debtors?

Look at how you can make your processes better

My definition of a good process is one that is easy to follow, gets the right result and feels natural. Currently I have good processes for remembering the children's lunchboxes but shocking processes for remembering to take the keys out of the ignition (thank you roadside assistance: twice in one week).

In a business sense, many of our processes simply evolve, and the lack of thought this entails can mean they end up clumsy, dubious or, like my car-key fiasco, dangerously hopeless.

So here's a little spring-clean for your processes.

What you need
- Your current processes.
- A bit of imagination.
- A desire to be organised.

What you do

The first step is to look at the processes you have in place and make a list of all the steps that could be improved.

To do this, read through your notes from the previous recipe and ask yourself:

- ❖ What can you do better?
- ❖ How can you do this better?
- ❖ Why do you do this at all?
- ❖ Where do you make mistakes?
- ❖ Which areas take longer than they should?
- ❖ Where are you wasting time?
- ❖ If you were starting afresh, what would you do differently?

The second step is to think about how you can improve your processes generally. To do this, write down the specific steps that go really well and ask yourself:

- ❖ What is it about these jobs that makes them easy to do?
- ❖ Why do you like doing those jobs?

And then do the same with the really awful steps that you procrastinate over and do appallingly:

- ❖ What is it about these jobs that makes them so terrible?
- ❖ Why do you hate these jobs?

See if there is a pattern emerging. Good processes often have very simple attributes, such as a fixed time to do them—'I always chase my debtors on Tuesday morning'—or a simple reminder—a 'checklist of things to confirm before I send the order out'. If your process is undemanding you will breeze through it.

But to be undemanding for *you* it needs to fit into your natural rhythms, which is why I suggest this bit of navel gazing.

So what about the steps that are going dreadfully? My guess is that these relate to areas that are quite simply not that interesting to you, or you don't know much about, or probably both. If this is the case, you are likely to need a bit of help.

Help comes in many different guises—you can ask your Owl (see chapter 12) and experts (see chapter 14)—and if you are quite clear about what problem it is that you are trying to solve, you will be amazed at who is willing to help. And for free.

Start by asking local businesses you work with. I can assure you they will be so flattered that they will give you chapter and verse on the mistakes they have made and what they do now. And if you ask a selection of businesses you will get some really great ideas.

What new processes do you need?

I am sure that I have used up my entire memory. It's the only explanation I can find for my recent 'forgetting-my-shopping' run.

It started when I left my husband's birthday present in the clothes shop and peaked last week when I left four bags of fruit and veg at the supermarket.

So I have implemented some controls into my shopping routine—every time I leave a shop I have to ask myself out loud if I have got all my bags.

It's getting me a bit of unwanted attention, but that's nothing compared to the humiliation I suffered a few years ago during my last forgetful streak when I forgot to put my skirt on!

What you need
❖ A gentle system of controls.

What you do
Controls are just processes that stop you making mistakes. Think control briefs for your business—they stop unwanted bulges of time and money.

To work out what controls you need (aside from girdle, bike shorts, camisole) think about these two questions:
❖ What can go wrong?
❖ What can you do to stop that happening?

Take each of your buying, doing and selling cycles from the first recipe and go through all the stages, asking 'What can go wrong?' Write it all down. Don't solve it yet—there is nothing like worrying about finding a solution to dampen your enthusiasm for finding problems.

Once you have done all three cycles, go back to your list of 'What can go wrong?' and now think of processes you could put in place to stop that happening. Make them nice and simple, using the earlier recipes as a guide. Here's a few examples to start you off.

WHAT CAN GO WRONG IN THE BUYING CYCLE

What can go wrong	Controls that may help
You place an order with your supplier but don't receive it	• Keep a file of unfulfilled orders. • Check the file on a weekly basis and follow up all orders that are due.
You receive a short order	• Check all orders as soon as they arrive. • Note the error on the supplier's 'goods delivery note'. • Call the supplier immediately and get an amended invoice. • Check all invoices to your 'Goods Received' note before entering them into the accounting system.
You pay the same invoice twice	• Match the invoice with the order and Goods Received note before paying. • Stamp as paid. • File in a 'Paid Invoice' file.

What can go wrong	Controls that may help
You forget to pay the invoice and get blacklisted by the supplier	• Enter all purchase invoices into the accounting system as soon as they are received. • File unpaid invoices in an 'Unpaid Invoices' file. • Check through the Unpaid Invoices file and the creditors ledger (from your accounting package) once a week.

SageCo

Alison Monroe, Catriona Byrne and Margaret Seaberg formed a friendship working together at the Sydney Olympics that would see them embark on a marathon of their own: SageCo. Quite aside from their great story about processes, these ladies have opened my eyes to the wonderful world of wisdom workers.

Among many other services, SageCo helps organisations set up processes to capture all the stuff in the heads of their mature-age employees before they retire.

Says Alison, 'We were the first people to do this and it seems we struck a nerve because we were overwhelmed with demand. We were very, very busy. In fact I would say that we were close to collapsing in a heap from exhaustion. The answer of course was to do like the good doctor, and take a swig of our own medicine. But we literally had to force ourselves to make the time to do it. It's hard, when you are so busy working with clients, to take time out and work on your own business, but it is essential. Somehow we found the time and worked on setting up our own watertight systems and processes. And it was worth it. We turned our know-how into a process—embracing technologies such as wiki and mind-mapping software—hired a team of employees to service our clients, and basically freed ourselves up to grow the business.'

The result? A business that is simply sprinting ahead.

Visit SageCo at www.sageco.com.au.

Christmas Cake

This fruitcake is lovely on its own, but feel free to ice it if you prefer.

WHAT YOU NEED

200 g butter
200 g dark brown sugar
2 tbsp golden syrup
1 tbsp marmalade
4 eggs, lightly beaten
225 g plain flour

$^{1}/_{2}$ tsp mixed spice
$^{1}/_{2}$ tsp ground cinnamon
800 g mixed dried fruit
100 g mixed peel
150 g glacé cherries
4 tbsp brandy

WHAT YOU DO

Preheat the oven to 150°C and line an 18 cm square cake tin. In a large bowl, cream the butter and sugar until light and fluffy, then mix in the syrup and marmalade. Slowly add the eggs, then fold in the flour. Mix in the remaining ingredients except the brandy.

Pour the mixture into the tin and bake for 3 hours. Turn out onto a wire rack and, once cool, make a few holes in the cake with a skewer and pour the brandy over.

14

BUY HELP: THE CHRISTMAS CAKE RECIPES

*C*hristmas for me is steeped in wintry English tradition: mulled wine, Christmas pudding, mince pies, turkey, and most of all, Christmas cake. When I was growing up my family was obsessed with Christmas cake, and every November we made an enormous one. My mum was chief cake maker, my sister and I were kitchen hands (washer-uppers paid in cake-bowl lickings) and my gran, who was later rewarded with the biggest slice, was on call as the 'is it cooked?' expert.

I have to confess that I take the easy option now and simply buy a cake. It costs a bit more but as I'm time-challenged and not a great Christmas-cake baker, it makes perfect sense to give the task to someone else. I did once try the packet-mix alternative, which is a sort of halfway house between doing it yourself and getting someone else to do it for you. It certainly saved time but I still had the awful responsibility of judging whether it was cooked—a fear which, it seems, I inherited from my mum.

The recipes in this chapter are about buying in help for your business in much the same way as my mother enlisted help for the annual Christmas cake. Don't dismiss the mere thought of this on the grounds that it will be too costly. It needn't be. And anyway, cost is a funny thing. While you are fiddling about trying to get your computer to work and saving the expense of hiring a fix-it man you are costing your business dearly: you are not making sales, you are not growing your business, and you are not doing what you're good at.

Besides, sometimes you just need *help*. Overstretched, overtired and overworked, you will end up 'over' your business. So invest in an extra pair of hands when you need it and consider it an early Christmas present. Or simply a lifesaver.

And when you have a bit of spare time, do try my gran's Christmas cake—it's perfect for all year round.

SANTA'S LITTLE HELPERS

Take what you can get for free, but sooner or later you may need to buy some help. This chapter is about getting the right sort of help and making it actually work for you. It's an important point because if you're not careful you could end up, like me, in a clean-the-house-before-the-cleaner-comes scenario.

The three business options for buying in help are:

- hiring an expert
- hiring employees
- hiring a contractor or simply outsourcing.

The 'hiring an expert' recipe is quite straightforward, but the actual act of hiring an expert tends to be studiously avoided. I do think this is a shame as it can be money very well spent. After all, a little expert help can go a long way; armed with a nugget of advice you can probably do the rest yourself.

Even the thought of an employee—let alone the arrival of a *real person*—invokes terror in some people. If this sounds like you then you need to factor an employee-free zone into the sort of business you are growing. However for many kitchen table tycoons, hiring employees becomes a necessity: you simply cannot grow a business without them. So the employee recipes rather assume that you *do* want to have a little team in your business and, because the whole employee thing is fraught with anxiety, I am including six recipes on this vexing topic. Just skip over them if it's not for you.

If you want to avoid employees, how about getting someone else to do the work for you? Outsourcing is a great alternative to managing staff, especially if you don't have any skills in that area. And contractors—the guys that lie somewhere between employees and outsourcing—can be gems. I like to think of them as people who come into your business to help out on a specific project and then, blissfully, disappear again.

Hiring an expert

Thank you, Warren Buffett. Your quote 'Price is what you pay, value is what you get' has been very useful; even today I thought of you when justifying the instant replacement of a Jo Malone Pomegranate Noir candle on the basis of its enormous value to my personal wellbeing.

Seriously though, this legendary American businessman was imperative in marshalling my thoughts on the use of experts. Yes, they are pricey; yes, their hourly rates seem outrageous; yes, I worry that once they hook me on they will reel me in and I'll forever be a client—and yes, hurrah, I can see that they add enormous value to my business and are therefore not actually expensive.

What you need
- A very good reason for hiring an expert.
- A very good expert.

What you do

For the occasions when you simply don't have the necessary skills, experts save you enormous time and angst. But be prepared before you engage them.

BEFORE YOU LOOK FOR AN EXPERT

Write down:

- ❧ what you need their expertise for
- ❧ what you want their output to be
- ❧ what skills they need to have
- ❧ what your budget is.

WHERE TO LOOK FOR AN EXPERT

The world is awash with experts, but how do you find a good one?

- ❧ Ask your family and friends for referrals.
- ❧ Ask local business people—even if you don't know them very well, they won't mind telling you where they get their legal help and whether they are any good.
- ❧ Look out for good examples. You might like someone's website; it doesn't matter if you don't know them, just call them up and ask who their designer was.

HOW TO PICK AN EXPERT

Gut feeling counts for a lot, but give it some help by drawing up a short list of no fewer than three experts. Visit all three to explain what you are looking for, and give them a bit of an interrogation. If one mentions something important that you haven't thought of, phone the others back and ask them about it. Also, ask each one for:

- fee quotes, and on what basis that is prepared—is it a fixed fee for the project, or an estimate of time and materials?
- examples of some of their work
- examples of who they work with, particularly people like you
- an indication of how long the project will take
- permission to contact a couple of their clients so that you can check out how good they really are!

BEFORE YOU HIRE

- Be very specific about what you want help with.
- Be very clear about what you expect the expert's output to be.
- Negotiate the fees.
- Ask the expert for a written fee quote and engagement terms which you both sign.
- Read the engagement letter carefully and make sure you understand it.
- If it's going to be pricey, ask if you can pay by monthly instalments or, if appropriate, on a success fee basis.

- ❖ Ask your expert how you can keep the costs down (see the note on accountants below).
- ❖ Ask for a timetable.

DURING THE ENGAGEMENT

- ❖ Ask the expert to tell you how much any additional work will cost *before* they do it—then you can choose whether to partake in it.
- ❖ Remember experts are salespeople too—be sure that you actually need any extra help that they are offering.
- ❖ Nag them if they are taking too long.

EXAMPLE: COUNTING THE PENNIES

If you are working with an accountant, to keep costs down:
- ❖ tell them that you want to keep costs down and do as much yourself as possible
- ❖ ask them for a list of all the information they need so you can put it together in a neat, understandable package. If the information is incomprehensible or incomplete it will cost you more to get the job done
- ❖ at the end of the job, ask if there is anything you can do to make it easier for them (and cheaper for you) next time.

Employees: who should you be hiring?

Do you ever go window shopping? I don't mean just looking in shop windows at night, I mean the real deal: tantalising visits to shops where you know you can't buy anything but have great fun pretending that you can.

Before you even think about employing someone, I recommend a spot of window shopping for your business.

What you need
- A sprinkling of imagination.
- A healthy dose of thinking time.

What you do
This is fun. It's about working out what roles you need to fill in the business. And it's fun because you absolutely must not, even for one minute, think about how you are going to afford these employees. You are just window shopping.

Start by asking yourself:
- What are your skills?
- Where do you add most value to your business?
- What jobs do you hate doing?
- What jobs are you not very good at doing?
- Which jobs do you simply ignore?
- What roles are there in your business?

- What roles would you just love someone else to do?
- What roles do you really need help with?
- What could someone help you with that would turn your business around?

Then prioritise the jobs and roles—which ones do you really need to fill first?

And this is why window shopping is so important. When you look around to see what you like without worrying about budgets, you free yourself up to choose the best, most flattering pieces. When you only look at what you think you can afford, the temptation is to choose plenty of cheap pieces that, to be honest, never really fit quite right.

Employees: what are you looking for?

My 'I'll know it when I see it' shopping modus operandi seems to serve me very well and, being totally honest, has also worked perfectly in helping me select a job, a husband and a house.

But it has never found me the right employee. That's not to say that it hasn't helped uncover good potential employees. It has. It's just been singularly unsuccessful at throwing up the right person for the right business at the right time.

So my hiring MO is to know exactly what I am looking for before I start the search.

What you need

A well-thought-out job specification and picture of the employee-to-be, which sets out:

* the detailed role that you are hiring for—the responsibilities and tasks
* the skills you are looking for to fulfil that role
* characteristics the employee will need to have to fit into your business
* an idea of what role the next employee you hire will fulfil.

What you do

The 'who should I be hiring' recipe is a good base for your job specification, but you need to pad it out with detail. And be really honest about the role you are hiring for—you won't believe the number of employee-princesses who simply refuse to get down and dirty.

Being specific about the role will help you in the future too—to manage your employee's performance. Especially useful if a princess slips through the net.

Now it's very possible that you won't really know what skills your employee needs to have to fulfil her role. If that's the case, ask your Owl or an expert. Your accountant, for example, will be happy to tell you the skills required by a bookkeeper.

You will want to make sure that your employee's personality fits the culture of your business. Skills can be learned, but personalities don't change. And think about what is most important to you—will you pick qualifications over experience; energetic youth over rock-solid middle age; or a chatterbox over silence?

Employees: where will you find them?

Last week I stumbled over an exceptionally audacious mum.

This mum, on finding herself between nannies, hangs out in play parks studying the carers of other children. When she spots what looks like a good nanny she charms her in conversation, entices her with money, advises her how to leave her current job without giving ample notice and then employs her on the spot.

All tactics that I guess she learned when her second husband wooed her from her first.

What you need
* A very clear idea of what you are looking for.
* A wee bit of chutzpah.

What you do
Fabulous roles rarely find their way to the job pages—instead they are advertised through networks and snapped up by friends of friends. You must do the same.

Yes, you can advertise, but you have to tell an incredibly compelling story about your business to be heard above the noise of all the other adverts. And yes, you can use recruitment consultants, but they are not a cheap option.

So I suggest that you turn poacher. Well it's not really poaching, is it? It's just giving someone the opportunity of a better job. So as long as you aren't doing anything illegal or truly immoral, go ahead and poach someone.

Use your imagination. Think creatively. Many small businesses hire university students for part-time work—brains and enthusiasm at lowish prices. And what about oldies: baby-boomers leaving big companies wanting to carry on working in some capacity could bring you a stunning injection of grey-haired wisdom.

Employees: how will you woo them on a small budget?

So you've just started dating a tall, good-looking guy. It's all going really well, you go back to his house and he...kicks off his 6-inch stacked heels! How do you feel? Disappointed. Cheated. Misled.

It's the same deal with your business. When it comes to attracting employees, don't try to hide the fact that you are a little outfit. Instead be bold and proud of your stature. And remember that the best things come in small packages.

What you need

- ❖ To be a seller.
- ❖ To tell a story.
- ❖ To spell out the opportunities.
- ❖ To offer something more valuable than cash.

What you do

Do what you do best: sell the story of your business, wrap it in 'what's in it for me, the potential employee?' packaging and tie it up with an opportunity they can't resist.

BE A SELLER

Instead of picturing yourself as buying an in-demand employee, think of yourself as selling a rare opportunity: a job in your business.

In 'buying' mode you put yourself into a competition about price, and the anxiety you feel about being strapped for cash will seep out. In 'selling' mode you will just ooze passion for your amazing business and appear much more confident and engaging.

TELL A STORY

Tell your employees-to-be a compelling story about your business and yourself. Think of your story as:

- how your business is changing a piece of the world
- how your product solves somebody's problem
- how your employee-to-be can contribute to your business's purpose.

And because people don't actually work for businesses—they work for people—make sure you give off the right vibes as well. You want to subtly let your potential employees know that you are a motivational and enthusiastic boss.

SPELL OUT THE OPPORTUNITIES

All employees are looking for roles that stimulate and challenge them, and as a small growing business you have an enormous advantage over the office cubicle. It is simply impossible to work in a small business and not get involved in diverse and challenging projects—you just need to spell that out to your employees-to-be.

OFFER SOMETHING MORE VALUABLE THAN CASH

Flexibility is hard to come by in the corporate world, but if you can organise your business to accommodate 10 a.m. to 2 p.m. roles you will never be short of reasonably priced and exceptionally talented mums.

Be creative with how you reward your employees and give them a piece of the action. If you set their base salary lower than market level but promise to top it up with a great bonus when the business does well, you will attract employees who really believe that they can help your business succeed. And, of course, because you only pay the bonus if the business is going well, you will be able to afford it. Perfect.

Employees: picking 'the one'

I hired an assistant because she reminded me of my best friend, and a nanny because she looked cuddly. Suffice to say, looks are a terrible screening method.

What you need
* Resumes.
* Interviews.
* References.

What you do
Ask for resumes, and read them. Do them all in one go so you can compare candidates. And look for what's missing, like mystery periods of 'no' employment.

Sparkle in your interviews, and:

- before you start, write down the questions you are going to ask
- ask all interviewees the same questions so that you can compare answers
- write down the responses and give them a mark out of 10—that way when you have finished the interviews you will remember who was who
- be honest—the interview is a two-way process. You want to see if the person is a good fit for you, but you also want the interviewee to know whether your business is a good fit for them
- be in selling mode. You are not just selling your job but selling your business. Every person you interview will talk about you afterwards—just make sure they say the right things
- let them do the talking
- think about asking them back for a second interview or a one-day trial. Makes the process a bit longer, but all worth it when you hire the right person.

And always check references because some potential employees are a bit economical with the truth. If you are in any doubt, don't hire.

When you do find the right person, get all the formal stuff done properly and have an expert cast their eye over it. As a minimum you should do a formal employment contract—and don't forget to include a probationary period, just in case.

Employees: keeping the magic alive

And what happens when the gloss wears off your shiny new relationship? How do you stay in love?

What you need
- ❖ To treasure your employees.

What you do
You are not neurotic—everyone is worried about investing time and self in their employees only to see them down tools and go and work for someone else. And it's not all about money; in fact it's often not about money at all.

Here are a few things that your employees want that won't cost you a bean.

- ❖ Career progression—the smallest businesses have the most amazing opportunities for employees; you just need to help your staff see them.
- ❖ Training—everyone likes to learn new things. This doesn't have to mean expensive training courses; on-the-job training is just as valuable.
- ❖ Feedback—employees desperately want to improve; help them by giving them feedback on their performance.
- ❖ A pat on the back—everyone loves to feel appreciated.

❧ Goals—everyone loves the satisfaction of achieving goals, so set some measurable targets for your employees.

Treasure your employees, but don't let them treat you poorly. If someone isn't pulling their weight, take action. Some employees, like most children, need boundaries—they need to know how far they can push you.

How to avoid hiring employees

If you are reeling from the thought of having employees, there are two alternatives. Both are delicious in their own way.

What you need
❧ Option 1: a contractor.
❧ Option 2: someone to outsource to.

What you do
You can consider hiring a contractor, or you could outsource your work.

Contractors are people you use for help on a specific project; usually you pay them an hourly rate for the work they do. You tell them what you want done and they do it. (My cleaner is a contractor. I, very nicely of course, tell her what to do and she does it.) Best of all, you only use them when you need them. But there is a downside—sometimes you can't find one when you need one.

Outsourcing your work means passing the whole kit and caboodle onto someone else so you don't have to get involved in any of the detail. This can be quite a relief—or, if you are a control freak, rather stressful. I outsource my ironing to John-The-Ironing-Man (I *so* detest ironing). He tells me what to do—'leave the washing on the step'—and I do it.

I don't have a housekeeper, but (wishful thinking here) if I did she would probably be an employee.

Small note here—tax people get very excited about the difference between contractors and employees. Speak to your accountant about that; this recipe is about how you and your help interact, not the Tax Act.

Finally, a word on accountability. While finding someone else to do the jobs that you can't (or don't want to) do gets the work done, it unfortunately doesn't absolve you from all responsibility. So irrespective of whether you hire a bookkeeper to update your records or do the job yourself, it is your business and you are ultimately accountable for the accuracy of your financial information.

quick bites

If you think you can't afford help then consider this.

Let's say your skills are in selling, and you calculate that every hour you spend selling generates you one customer, and each customer gives you an average profit of $100.

Now you could spend five hours a week on bookkeeping, which would cost you $5 \times \$100 = \$500$ in lost profit.

On the other hand, you could employ a bookkeeper at $30 an hour. She is quicker at bookkeeping than you, so it only takes her three hours. Cost = $90. Hiring a bookkeeper is cheaper to your business by $\$500 - \$90 = \$410$.

Why wouldn't you do it?

quick bites

Finally, what if you're reluctant to employ someone because you just don't like people? I am going to be blunt here and say that running a business is probably not the best avenue for you. Businesses are about people—both as employees and customers. If you have a great idea for a business but really would rather hibernate away, consider hiring someone to actually *run* the business while you get on with the product development side.

Messenger Group

Lisa Messenger founded and runs the successful Messenger Group—a collaboration of creative companies—and she sums this chapter up perfectly.

'There are pros and cons to having employees and using experts,' Lisa says. And she would know. Over the past seven years in business she has experienced both ends of the spectrum. 'For the first three years of my business it was largely only me, and sometimes me and one other. I was absolutely passionate about the business and loved what I was doing but I was overservicing and undercharging and really hadn't tapped into the collective wisdom of experts who had trodden the path before me. In essence, for each client I was reinventing the wheel with no defined systems or processes, and working around the clock trying to be everything to everyone. Lots of fun but certainly not sustainable. The business was completely reliant on me and I was really just trading time for money, which was both exhausting and certainly no way to get rich.'

Lisa says that once they became really clear about their vision they were able to maintain focus and the business just grew practically overnight. 'We started to understand the power of PR and surrounding ourselves with mentors, business coaches and other business owners. We had a really solid business offering with a real point of difference, little competition and a ready market and we just blossomed.

'Taking on extra staff meant we were able to really leverage ourselves to the maximum and the business was no longer solely reliant on me. Not only did we suddenly find ourselves with a lot of internal staff (which can often be demanding), where the real leverage occurred was using the services of a host of external freelancers and contractors, allowing us to create teams on a needs basis.

'I'm now pleased to say that I have a pretty good grasp of it and am not ashamed to admit to what I don't know. I have become the queen of coming up with great, creative ideas and surrounding myself with a fabulous team who can make it all happen.

'This allows me and my core management team the flexibility to continue to keep the creative skills and the operational side of the business functional, while having lots of support from people who are the experts in their domain.'

Visit the Messenger Group at www.messengermarketing. com.au.

Part V

TIPPING THE SCALES IN YOUR FAVOUR

If you have ever embarked on a weight loss program you will know that the theory is simple enough—eat less and exercise more—but that *doing* it is hard. Very hard.

Much of your success will hinge on motivation: are you willing to forgo an ice cream today to look like a wafer in three months' time? And of course some of your success will depend on genetics—I'm no dietitian but it seems pretty obvious to me that not all bodies respond in the same way to the calories-in/effort-out ratio. The best motivation is seeing results. And I don't mean the my-skirt-feels-looser wishful-thinking type of results but the real, can't-be-manipulated ones. Like the bathroom scales.

Baking a business has a lot in common with weight management. You start with a goal and bake a series of nutritionally balanced recipes to achieve it. Success depends on your ability to keep motivated—it only works if you keep up the effort—and business type: quite simply, some businesses respond better to nourishment than others. And in terms of a source of motivation—and a guide to how your business reacts to sustenance—you really can't beat results. So that is what this final section is all about.

I like to think of this section as a weight management program for your business. Fortunately you have already done much of the work—you are laden with goals and nutritious recipes—so this final hurrah focuses on how you actually measure your results. It's rather like building bathroom scales for your business . . . but remember you do actually have to *stand* on them.

Rich Ginger Flapjacks

This recipe is proof, if you needed it, that you can get great taste with minimum effort and without paying attention to detail. You don't even have to get the quantities right—they are just there as a guide.

WHAT YOU NEED

85 g butter or margarine

60 g Demerara sugar

1 tbsp golden syrup

120 g rolled oats

½ level tsp ground ginger

WHAT YOU DO

Preheat the oven to 170°C and grease an 18 cm sandwich cake tin.

Melt the butter with the sugar and syrup in a saucepan and pour onto the mixed rolled oats and ginger. Mix well, put the mixture into the prepared tin, press down firmly and bake for 35 minutes. Cut into fingers when cool.

15

Getting results: the Weigh-Up recipes

*Y*ou have to grab the bull by the horns in the first recipe in this chapter and dig out your accounting records. Now I appreciate that even the slightest mention of accounting stuff may leave you feeling a bit glum. But don't let it: the whole point about the weigh-up program is that you only need your accounting stuff to work out your starting point. Then you can manage, to a certain extent, without it.

Before I raise the ire of accountants and tax inspectors everywhere I should make it clear that I am not, for one minute, suggesting that you dispense with your accounting records completely. You need them for tax and legal reasons and, more than that, they are jam-packed with information and are brilliant.

But sometimes you don't need brilliant. Sometimes all you really want is a few key bits of information. Sometimes you just want to jump on the scales and see what you weigh rather than get out the fat callipers, tape measure and water-retention percentages.

Of course the other problem with accounting records is keeping them up to date; I empathise with you here. With all this in mind these weigh-up techniques are based on rough and ready information, rather than minutely accurate accounting reports. So I urge you to feel comfortable about getting your accounting records out in step one, because it's the only time you will need them.

The second recipe is about setting your target size. This isn't about being particularly big or small, it's about a profit figure that will fit in with your needs and your lifestyle. Converting your target size in the third recipe is simple enough to understand, but it can be a little tricky to do. In essence it is the business equivalent of converting dress size 10 (your target size) into 55 kg (your target weight). The final three recipes are about making it work in practice.

Here are the weigh-up recipes.

- Size your business up right now.
- Set your target size.
- Convert your target size into weight.
- Determine your profit-driver targets.
- Tips for making it work.

- Taking action.
- What if it's all pear-shaped?

I can't say any more, except to implore you to do the weigh-up program. It gets results, it motivates...it's the icing on the cake.

Size your business up right now

Have you ever tried very hard to not notice that you are getting fatter? Have you blamed too-tight jeans on the tumble-dryer and censured your favourite shop for down-sizing their 12s? Googled 'water retention' and obsessed over dandelion tea, and flatly refused to own a set of bathroom scales?

Now it is time to face the truth.

What you need
- Your most recent profit figure.

What you do
Start by asking yourself what the term 'size' actually means to you: what do you want to grow? For most people the answer to this is profit, so that is the gauge I have used in this and subsequent recipes. But you can just as easily substitute revenue, cash, or whatever takes your fancy.

It really doesn't matter what profit figure you use to start with, as long as you feel it is fairly accurate. So if the most recent information you have is for the financial year that ended six months ago, so be it; use that. But if you possibly can, it is worth having a go at getting your accounting records up to date to give you a good start. They don't have to be perfect, just a guide. I think it helps you get over 'business dysmorphic disorder' (a distorted image of what your business really looks like), which often manifests as a business that is in better shape in your imagination than it is in real life.

Finally, you will need to get a sense of your profit per week. To do this, just divide your profit by the number of weeks that it relates to.

Set your target size

I want to be a size 8, I want to be able to fit into my pre-pregnancy jeans, I want to be the size I was when I got married.

Everybody needs a target, a goal.

What you need
❖ A profit goal and/or any other goals that would be useful to you.

What you do

You did the confronting bit in the previous recipe; you sized yourself up. Now this is the fun bit where you get to say what size you would like to be in a year's time.

You might want to flick back to your 'Goals' recipe in chapter 12 to remind yourself what you want to achieve. And then phrase that in profit terms. You can do other goals too, but don't over-complicate it. The aim here is to make something simple and well done, rather than intricate and half-baked.

You may be unsure what it is possible to achieve, but if you set targets (drop a dress size) and track your progress, you have a very good chance of getting there, irrespective of where 'there' is.

Now, in this recipe I suggest you look at your target profit for a whole year because I think that will give you enough time to see some real changes. If you don't like a year, just pick whatever time period makes sense to you.

Finally, in much the same way that you did in the earlier recipe, calculate a target profit per week. I do realise that your profit is unlikely to be earned equally through the year, so you may feel that just dividing profit by the number of weeks isn't exactly representative of real life. But relax: this is just to get a feeling of your weekly profit.

Once done, compare your current weekly profit from the previous recipe with your target one. How big is the gap? Do you feel it is enough of a stretch? Do you think it is possible?

If the answer to any of these questions is 'no', rework your target until you are happy with it.

Tip: Your goals need to be ones that are really important to you. Setting a goal of, say, $1 million in revenue for the year is great if that is what you are really interested in. Remember, there are plenty of businesses with big revenues and tiny profits. Revenue gives you only braggability, not spendability.

Convert your target size into weight

Have you ever tried measuring yourself with a tape measure? You can honestly get any answer that you want. Feeling a bit fat? Just tighten the tape measure to get a smaller reading.

But there is nowhere to hide when you are standing naked on the scales.

If you don't like the answer on the scales you can try again tomorrow (just don't eat a big dinner tonight), try again next week (when your PMS bloating will be over), try standing differently on the scales (lean over to the left a bit and try to outsmart the technology), or try standing on your friend's scales (just be careful with the nudity bit).

But in all probability your scales will be pretty much right.

What you need

❖ To understand the key profit drivers in your business.

What you do

This recipe is slightly tricky, but absolutely worth getting to grips with.

If you want to shrink from a size 14 to a size 10 you are actually trying to change your body measurements—boobs, tum, hips—but because it's hard to tape-measure yourself accurately each week (and even remotely discern any progress), you probably just weigh yourself.

It's the same principle here for your business. It's time consuming and tricky to get an accurate profit figure out of your accounting reports daily or weekly. That's because some of your costs won't exactly match up with what you are doing now—you may have paid your rent a quarter in advance, or just bought enough packaging to last you for the whole year—and it's quite a job to make the necessary adjustments for this every week. So, like measuring weight rather than centimetres, I am going to suggest that you measure something other than profit.

The *something else* goes by the name of your 'profit driver', and it is probably easiest explained by way of this example.

Say you run a club. The costs are pretty much fixed in advance so you can only increase profit by increasing revenue. An increase in revenue could be achieved by increasing the membership fees or increasing the number of members. But because you have set the membership fee at the beginning of the year, you know that the only thing that can change your profit is your member numbers. So rather than trying to measure profit each week, you only need to measure the number of members. And you don't even have to measure the total number of members, just the net new members (joiners less leavers). In other words, your profit driver in this example would be net new members.

So, profit drivers are those bits of your business that, when they change, have the biggest impact on it. What you need to do now is work out what yours are. You really don't want too many, just two or three.

If you have a simple, easy-to-understand business model (see chapter 5) then you will be able to identify your profit drivers quite quickly. And if you're not sure whether something is a driver, ask yourself whether focusing on it will give you the results you want.

Tip: Creating a budget (chapter 9) and regularly comparing your actual costs with your planned ones will take care of your anxieties about overhead costs so you can set your profit driver to focus simply on revenue and gross profit.

Determine your profit-driver targets

This is the vexing question of 'how do you know what a size 10 looks like in kilos?'

What you need

❖ To convert profit 'size' targets into driver 'weight' targets.

❖ To build some scales to weigh the drivers.

What you do

If you have been working through the recipes in this section, by now you will know your current profit, target profit and profit drivers. So this recipe is just about converting your hard-to-measure profit target into an easy-to-measure profit driver.

It is a bit like converting your goal of being a size 10 into a target weight of, say, 55 kg. Again, I think it is best explained by an example. So, thinking about the club in the previous recipe, if you want to increase profit by $100,000 for the year, and you know that new memberships yield a profit of $200 each, then your target driver (net new members) will be 500.

As well as having a target driver for the year, I also suggest that you have a weekly one. Compare the prospect of trying to lose 50 kg with the goal of losing 1 kg a week for a year. The latter seems so much more doable.

Armed with your target, the only thing you need to do now is build the scales to measure it. And this should be quite straightforward. In the example of the club, the scales are the database (glorified word for spreadsheet) which details the number of new members; your business will have something similar. Remember to make it easy.

Tips for making it work

We all lie to ourselves a little bit; I think it's a natural defence mechanism. In weight loss it's akin to remembering your weight at its lowest and dismissing upward movements as aberrations.

What you need
- ✻ A weekly 'weigh-in'.
- ✻ Driver diaries.
- ✻ A 'traffic light' report.

What you do
Get into the habit of giving your business a weekly 'weigh-in'.

Of course this is easy to do when you are expecting good news, but tempting to avoid when you are not. My suggestion is that you create a 'driver diary' where you record your profit driver measurements each week. I do this on a simple spreadsheet.

The next logical step is to compare your weekly driver measurement with your target driver from a few recipes back. If you have underperformed against your target, don't despair; just figure out the reason why.

I like to take the driver diary one step further and turn it into a 'traffic light' report. Even though this involves just colour-coding the results, I find it makes for a far more fun and comprehensible read. So what you do is this: if you hit target for the week, colour the diary entry green in your spreadsheet. If you almost hit it, colour it amber, and if you fail to hit it, colour it red. A page of green cells will motivate you, a sea of amber cells will make you 'up the ante' a bit, and a swathe of red cells will alarm you into action.

Once you have got the hang of this you can play around with it a bit more. A good addition to the diary is a 'results-to-date' column. To do this, simply add up your driver results since the beginning of the year and compare it with the total of your weekly targets for the same period. You can traffic-light this too and it will give you a better sense of how you are tracking.

You can download a traffic light report from www. thebusinessbakery.com.au.

Taking action

It's all very well having a target, but how are you actually going to make it happen? Perhaps, eat less, exercise more. But less of what, and what is less?

No wonder we love a 'diet'. A diet tells us how much to eat (calories/points/fat globules), gives us recipes for tasty food (where a portion size fits on one spoon) and shouts at us to run around the park.

What you need
❖ To take action.
❖ To keep a diary of your actions.

What you do
Intentions are nothing unless you actually turn them into actions. So now is the time to decide what activities you are going to undertake to improve your profit. And start doing them. The recipes in this book provide some suggestions; you will have other ideas yourself, and if you still need more inspiration visit www.thebusinessbakery.com.au.

Stick slavishly to your regular weigh-ins. That is the only way to know for sure whether the recipes are working. If you aren't getting the desired outcome, maybe it's early days (some recipes, like exercise, take more than a few weeks to make an impact), or maybe you haven't been as diligent in applying the recipes as you thought.

And a quick word of caution: don't try too many new things at once. It will be hellish trying to figure out what's working for you and what's not.

Finally, you might want to consider keeping a diary of your activities. This works in the same way as a food diary by recording what you actually did, rather than what wishful thinking hoped you had done. Re-reading the diary can be very illuminating! Keeping a diary also helps if you are afflicted with a shortage of free memory, serving as a reminder of what you have changed and when (for example, the date that you increased prices) so that you can follow the impact through to your weigh-ins.

What if it's all pear-shaped?

It's grossly unfair, but sometimes you think you have done everything right and then you jump on the scales and your weight has gone up, not down!

There are a few things you can do. (My favourite is to buy new scales.)

What you need
* A clear head.

What you do

I'm almost serious about buying new scales.

If you simply don't believe what the scales are telling you, check the scales. Your scales are the systems and processes that are producing your weekly profit driver figure. If the numbers don't seem to stack up, maybe there are some problems with your system. So first up, check that you haven't made any silly mistakes (we all make them, believe me). If your processes are letting you down, flick back through chapter 13.

If you are pretty sure your scales are telling you the truth, think back over the last week/month. What has been different? Sometimes we overlook the simple things. You may weigh more because it's that-time-of-the-month bloating; you may be selling less because of seasonal effects on sales.

Healthy Habits

Passionate about a healthy alternative to the standard quick-bite fare, Katherine Sampson founded Healthy Habits. It started as one sandwich bar, then two, then three, then . . . well, then she realised that she couldn't operate lots of sandwich outlets herself. So she franchised the concept into the popular Healthy Habits food retail chain.

Katherine's flair is in marketing, innovation and sales, and she is the first to say that the 'numbers bit' is her Achilles heel. But when the business was small it didn't matter, says Katherine: 'When I just had the one shop I knew my profit drivers intimately. I didn't have to worry about costs too much because I knew that the key to my business was to maximise volume, minimise waste.'

As the business grew, the numbers side became far more complex and Katherine was happy to hand it over—lock, stock and barrel—to someone else to manage. 'In hindsight that was probably a mistake. At first I was delighted not to have to worry about the numbers side, but hey, I'm running a business, I need to know and understand the figures.'

What Katherine's story illustrates is the importance of keeping an eye on your figure and taking action before your skirt starts to feel too tight. Figuring out the best way to do this, and acknowledging that numbers may not be your thing, is as good a place to start as any.

So Katherine brought in a new accountant to work alongside her. 'My accountant keeps all the nitty-gritty detail; I can keep on top of the business by just looking at key figures: our profit drivers. We sat down together to work out what our profit drivers actually are and now my accountant gives me the figures in that format. I can't be doing with too much more; I lose focus.'

The latest creation from Healthy Habits is a truly healthy alternative to the usual kids' junk food, and in a way is mirrored inside her business too. 'My strength may be in sales and marketing, but looking at my weekly numbers is my healthy habit,' says Katherine.

Visit Healthy Habits at www.healthyhabits.com.au.

LAST WORDS

I wanted to finish with a word about you.

In essence this is a short reminder to look after the most important part of your business: you. And I say this because it is so easy to get swept away by the urgency and immediacy of the little demon you have created and simply neglect your own wellbeing. You may have already experienced the slip into business martyrdom and felt the swell of pride as you recount how you are too busy to go to the gym, eat a decent meal and get more than a few hours' sleep a night.

But is that what you really wanted out of the business, and is it what the business really wants out of you? My guess is no.

So, for what it's worth, this is my advice. I am not a health nut but I do know that I have my best ideas when I go for a long walk, that I have much more energy when I eat food that bears some resemblance to the way that nature created it, and that I sleep better if I stop working at least half an hour before

I go to bed. I try to remember that caffeine is not the answer to lack of sleep and that shouting at the kids is not a good response to a business crisis. And I believe that cupcakes have magical properties, that a massage cures all ills, that yoga feels good and that the odd glass of wine is medicinal.

And finally, if you are working at home dressed in breakfast-encrusted leggings and a less-than T-shirt, and a cantankerous supplier calls, simply slip on your highest heels and strut around the house. It never fails to redress the balance of power.

Enjoy your business.

THE PANTRY

*Y*ou can start a business with very little in the way of know-how, and run a fine one with absolutely nothing in the way of terminology. But if you are interested, here is an explanation of some of the words that I have used in this book, some of the phrases that I didn't use but probably should have, and some extra useful bits and bobs.

Accounting gathering: Collecting together all the financial information into one place so that you don't forget any of it. Think in-trays and files.

Accounting package: There are two main bits to your accounting system—the stuff that happens outside the computer, and the stuff that happens inside the computer. Your accounting package is the stuff that happens inside the computer. It doesn't do magic and it's only as good as the ingredients that you put into it.

Accounting records: All the stuff stored in your accounting package and all the original documentation.

Accounting system: This is just the whole business of gathering up all your financial stuff (like your purchase invoices) and sorting it into something that makes sense.

Balance sheet: A summary of your assets and liabilities. It will tell you what your working capital and net assets are.

Cash book balance: Your cash book balance is quite simply the cash figure from your accounting reports. It is often different to the figure that is displayed when you do a bank balance enquiry because the latter is always a little bit out of date. And that's nothing to do with the bank being slow but rather because suppliers may not have presented their cheques yet, lodgements may still be being processed, or because the cheque really is in the post!

Coding: This is the really important bit if you want your computer to spit out accounting information that is useful. You need to put your information into the computer in a certain way by giving it a code. Your accounting package will tell you the codes to give, but remember that if you want to track your costs cleverly you need to code them appropriately and consistently.

Debtors: The people who owe you money.

Direct costs: The costs that, in a biscuit business, you only incur if you make a batch of biscuits. It's the stuff that relates directly to the biscuit-making process, like materials, manufacturing, packaging, distribution and the costs of warehousing.

Distribution costs: These are all the costs of getting your product from where it first originated to the place where your customer gets it. So, in a biscuit business, your distribution costs will include the costs of getting the flour, eggs, butter and yummy chocolatey bits to the manufacturer, and then the costs of getting the biscuits from the manufacturer to your warehouse, and then on to the retail outlet that will sell them. Some of these costs will be obvious as they appear on an enormous invoice. Others you will need to think about and calculate. If you are driving the bikkies around in your car to all the local cafes you have petrol costs and a cost for your time, not to mention the wear and tear on your car. It may be quite tricky working out the distribution cost per biscuit, but you do need to do it (add up all the costs and divide by the average number of biscuits transported . . . or how many biscuits the flour will make). Don't worry if you can't be exact: a good estimate is a lot more worthwhile than not bothering at all!

Financial model: A slightly off-putting name for your financial food processor.

Gross profit and net profit: Gross profit is your Big Fat Profit, which is calculated as your revenue less your direct costs. Net profit is the minuscule amount that is left when you take your overheads away from your gross profit.

Inputting: This is just typing your financial information into the computer. As long as you don't make any typos and you follow your coding, it's easy as.

Key performance indicators: In business speak, profit drivers (chapter 15) are also called key performance indicators or KPIs. They are just the thing you measure to gauge how your business is performing.

Leverage: A funny term which simply means using your time and money in a clever way so that you get a better outcome. It's just another term for double dipping.

Manufacturing costs: This might be obvious—the amount the manufacturer charges you. It is less obvious if you are making stuff yourself with your own employees. If this is the case you will need to work out how many hours are involved in cooking up a batch of biscuits, and then what the hourly rate of you and your staff is. You will then need to work out how to spread that cost over the number of biscuits that you made in that batch to work out the manufacturing cost per biscuit. (So if it takes five hours at $20 per hour to make 100 biscuits, each biscuit costs $1 to make.)

Materials costs: This is pretty obvious—it's the flour, the sugar, the egg, the melt-in-your-mouth chocolate. And because the amounts are measured fairly accurately you will be able to cost the materials per item. (So if 1 kg sugar costs $10 and makes 100 biscuits, the sugar for each biscuit costs 10 cents.)

Net assets: These are all the assets of the business, less all the liabilities of the business. It's different to working capital because that just includes the assets that are going to turn into cash soon. Net assets include everything—even fixed assets like your car and furniture and computer equipment. Bits and bobs that you have no intention of selling. It also includes liabilities you don't have to pay out in cash soon—like a long-term loan with the bank.

If your net assets are a big fat minus you are in a pickle. It means that the business owes more than it can ever collect in cash. You need to work out how you are going to be able to settle all your debts. If you don't think you can, see an accountant or your bank manager quickly.

Net profit: See gross profit.

Overheads: All the other costs that hang about, like rent and accounting fees.

Packaging costs: All the funky packaging you found to entice potential customers also comes with a cost. And sometimes it's a big one. You will need to calculate a 'per biscuit' price for this, but you might find the answer a bit clunky. Packaging is a very important part of how you market your stuff, but you need to keep on top of the cost.

Profit-and-loss account: A summary of your revenue and your costs, which comes down to a bottom-line figure of profit (yippee).

Reports: These are what the computer spits out (when you ask it to). All the computer does is take the information you have inputted, adds it to all the stuff you have inputted before and sorts it according to the coding you have given it. When you ask the computer for a report it just spits out the info again, but in a way that is meant to be useful to you.

Warehousing costs: These are the costs of storing your biscuits. You may be able to store them for free in your garage but let's say that you hire refrigeration space. You will need to calculate roughly how long you store the biscuits and how many you store at a time to work out a per-biscuit cost of storage. When you come to do the calculations you will probably find that the length of time and the number of biscuits 'just depends', so use your best estimate.

Working capital: This is the stuff that is going to turn into cash soon—it just hasn't quite got there yet—plus the cash in the bank. Basically it's your stock plus your debtors plus your cash less your creditors. Imagine that you owe your suppliers $10,000 and are worried about how you are going to pay it. You take a look at the business and see that you have $5000 of stock which you can sell, and $6000 of debts to collect. That's a total of $11,000 coming your way, so, phew, you know you are going to be able to pay your suppliers. Just not quite yet.

If your working capital is a big fat minus (so your creditors are way bigger than your cash plus your debtors and your stock), you might have a problem.

Acknowledgments

$\mathcal{T}$hank you to the wonderful women who have allowed me to share their stories: Jaime Halward, Naomi Simson, Paris Cutler, Carolyn Stafford, Doxia Dinoris, Paula Nemme, Sascha Griffin, Leone Martin, Margaret Butler, Nicole Mills, Sheila Ghosh, Jessica Eckford, Alison Monroe, Catriona Byrne, Margaret Seaberg, Lisa Messenger and Katherine Sampson. And thank you to my mother, Jan Culpitt, whose handwritten notebook, compiled over 40 years, is the source of the baking recipes.

Deepest thanks to Kristin Meagher for her judgment, friendship and unbridled enthusiasm. Thanks too to David Koch and Nigel Miller for involving me in *Kochie's Business Builders* and for introducing me to Paula Nemme, Leone Martin and Doxia Dinoris, all of whom appeared on the show. And many thanks to Jude McGee, Clara Finlay and the team at Allen & Unwin for publishing the book and making this whole experience so fun.

As someone who is enormously enthusiastic about starting projects but a lousy finisher I am indebted to the encouragement of all the friends who asked me, day in, day out, how the book was going. Quite simply, they made it too hard for me to give up.

But because it took me rather longer to write the book than I expected, and phenomenally longer than I had led my husband to believe, my biggest thanks must go to Mike for his love and support. Late one Friday night after a week when I had barely come up for air he did rather exasperatedly ask when the book would finally be finished. It is. Thank you.